SUGAR DETOX DIET

Easy Meal Plans and Healthy Everyday Recipes for Staying Sugar Free

(30 + Recipes to Satisfy Your Cravings)

Mary Campbell

Published by Alex Howard

© **Mary Campbell**

All Rights Reserved

Sugar Detox Diet: Easy Meal Plans and Healthy Everyday Recipes for Staying Sugar Free (30 + Recipes to Satisfy Your Cravings)

ISBN 978-1-990169-88-5

All rights reserved. No part of this guide may be reproduced in any form without permission in writing from the publisher except in the case of brief quotations embodied in critical articles or reviews.

Legal & Disclaimer

The information contained in this book is not designed to replace or take the place of any form of medicine or professional medical advice. The information in this book has been provided for educational and entertainment purposes only.

The information contained in this book has been compiled from sources deemed reliable, and it is accurate to the best of the Author's knowledge; however, the Author cannot guarantee its accuracy and validity and cannot be held liable for any errors or omissions. Changes are periodically made to this book. You must consult your doctor or get professional medical advice before using any of the suggested remedies, techniques, or information in this book.

Table of contents

Part 1 1
Introduction 2
Chapter 1: Breakfast-- A Champion's Start 4
Sweet Potato Frittata With Rosemary 5
Chia Seed Pudding 6
Breakfast Pizza 7
Egg And Ham Cups 8
Breakfast Burritos 9
Scrambled Eggs With Feta Cheese, Asparagus, And Smoked Salmon 10
Oatmeal Express 11
Cheddar, Turkey, And Guacamole Breakfast Sandwich 12
Chapter 2: Lunch-- Midday Fuel 13
Simple Crab And Pasta Salad 13
Tomato And Mozzarella Salad 15
Pineapple And Grilled Chicken Sandwich 16
Apricot Chicken With Beets 17
Garlic Shrimp Stuffed Avocado 18
Lamb Burgers And Mint Tzatziki 19
Shrimp Scampi 20
Quinoa With Figs, Peppers And Squash 22
Chapter 3: Dinner--Food For Thought 23
Beef Tenderloin With Mustard And Horseradish Crust 24
Feta And Spinach Stuffed Turkey Breast 26
Tuna Steaks With Lime Sauce And Avocado 29

Mexican Style Meatloaf 31
Greek Chicken Spaghetti 32
Cajun Scallops 33
Sausage And Peppers 34
Tangy Buffalo Chicken Pizza 35
Pork Tenderloin Medallions In Red Wine And Mushroom Sauce 36
Bonus Recipe: Cheesy Beef And Beet Crock Pot Chili 38
Chapter 4: Bonus Dessert Recipes 40
No Sugar Pumpkin Pie 40
Berry Burst Flan Tart 41
Cinnamon Vanilla Mousse 42
No Bake Pumpkin Cheesecake 43
No Bake Cherry Pie 45
Pineapple Milkshake 46
Melon Sorbet 47
Raspberry Icy Pops 48
Chocolate Coated Strawberry 49
Pecan Pie 50
Apple Muffins 51
Peanut Cookies 53
Coffee Cheesecake 55
Strawberry Sorbet 57
Walnut Cookies 58
Chocolate Maca Blast 60
Blueberry Cacao Blast 62
Raw Fudge 63

Blueberry Enchanting Muffins	65
Coconut Dates Balls	66
Strawberry Truffles	67
Chocolate And Banana Pudding	69
Cheery Cheesecake	71
Blackberry Cheesecake	73
Coconut Cheesecake	75
Honey And Lemon Cake	77
Strawberry Cake	79
Creamy Carrot Cake	81
Raspberry Pie	83
Pineapple Pie	85
Almond Cookies	87
Lemon Cupcakes	89
Strawberry Velvet Cupcake	91
Chapter 5: Sugar Free Cake And Pie Recipes	93
No Bake Strawberry Cheesecake	93
Apple Pie	95
Key Lime Pie	96
Strawberry Pie	98
Apple Raisin Cake	99
Banana Cake	101
Moist Chocolate Cake	102
Walnut Brownies	104
Blueberry Coffee Cake	106
Chocolate Pie	107
Chocolate Zucchini Cake	108

Chocolate Fudge Brownies 109
Pumpkin Pie 110
Coconut Cream Pie 110
Graham Cracker Chocolate Pie 111
Raisin Squares 112
Chapter 6: Sugar Free Cookies Recipes 114
Peanut Butter Cookies 114
Oatmeal Raisin Cookies 114
Snickerdoodles Cookies 115
Banana Oatmeal Cookies 116
Chewy Pecan Cookies 117
Cream Cheese Cookies 118
Pumpkin Cookies 119
Almond Cookies 120
Chocolate Chip Cookies 121
No Bake Peanutbutter Cookies 122
Chocolate Chip Coconut Cookies 122
Applesauce Cookies 123
Lemon Cookies 124
Walnut Raisin Cookies 125
Conclusion 127
Part 2 128
Introduction 129
Desserts With Sugar 130
Melt-In-Your-Mouth Brownies 130
White Cake 131
Italian Cream Cake 133

Chocolate Eclair Cake	135
Flourless Chocolate Cake	136
Crème Brulee	138
Chocolate Mousse	139
Madeleines	141
Fruit Clafouti	143
Tiramisu	144
Italian Cheese Cake:	146
German Apple Strudel	147
Baklava	149
Almond Cookies	151
Peach Cobbler	153
Strawberry Shortcake	154
Chocolate Soufflé	156
Pecan Pie	159
Coconut Cream Pie	160
Chocolate Gingerbread Cookies	162
Sugar-Free Desserts	164
Sugar Free Strawberry Cheesecake	164
Cinnamon Coffee Cake	165
Pumpkin Pie	167
Honey Cake	168
Chocolate Pie	169
Raspberry Custard	171
Funnel Cake	172
Banana Cake With Frosting	173
Peanut Butter Cookies	176

Fruit Mousse 177

Lemon Pie 178

Ginger Cookies 179

Coconut Truffles 180

Chocolate Lava Cake 182

Banana Nut Bread 183

Cherry Pie 185

Pineapple Upside-Down Cake 186

Shortbread Cookies 188

German Chocolate Cake .... **Error! Bookmark not defined.**

Apple Tart .... **Error! Bookmark not defined.**

Banana Nut Cake .... **Error! Bookmark not defined.**

Part 1

Introduction

When you have decided to quit sugar, it is normal that you will find mealtimes to be difficult, but likely the most challenging meal of the day to get through is going to be breakfast. In today's fast paced world where every second counts, more people are apt to have a bowl of sugary cereal, or swing by the drive through at the local donut shop than bother to cook something for themselves.

However, breakfast is the most important meal of the day. It gives your body the fuel that is required for the long day ahead. When **omitting sugar** is the goal, there is no rule that says only fruit or cereal are the best choices. Let imagination take the reins.

What is really important is to include **protein and healthy fats** in each meal. Learning to cook without adding sugar to any meal is really not difficult to do. It simply requires a little bit of self-discipline and a new way of doing things.

Even for those who are not gourmet chefs, there are so many recipes available for you to try that even if you were to experiment with a new one for every meal of the day, for the rest of your life, you would never run out of options. This is perhaps the most important thing since the majority of people tend to tire quickly of eating plans that lack variety.

Before long you will notice that eating sugar is often more of a habit than an actual need.

By eating well-balanced meals that are satisfying and filling, in a short period of time you will not even crave the taste of sugar. You will also find that you have more energy, are sick less often, and that any weight issues have stabilized.

And forgoing the sugar fix does not mean that you are in for a lifetime of meals that are tasteless and bland. I am going to give you a new start to a healthy, sugar-free way of eating with 25 recipes for breakfast, lunch, and dinner that are easy to make, use common ingredients, and are above all, totally delicious!

Thanks again for downloading this book, I hope you enjoy it!

Chapter 1: Breakfast-- A Champion's Start

There is no one who feels like dragging themselves out of bed in the morning and then spending hours making a proper breakfast. Likewise, there is no joyous rush to leave the comfort of your bed when all you have to look forward to is an unappetizing single egg white. Luckily, that is something that you do not have to worry about!

I am going to share some recipes for breakfast that taste great, do not require hours of your time, and will give you the proper balance of nutrients. There is going to be no compromising on taste with any of these 7 easy to prepare breakfast meals, and they can be customized to your individual likes and dislikes with no trouble. Enjoy!

Sweet Potato Frittata With Rosemary

Ingredients

8 eggs or egg whites

2 cups chopped sweet potatoes

1 tbsp rosemary

1 cup of spinach, finely chopped

Olive oil

Salt and pepper as desired

Directions

Roast sweet potatoes that have been tossed with rosemary and 1 tbsp olive oil in a 450° oven until soft and brown, about 40 minutes, occasionally stirring (can be prepared the evening before). Preheat a skillet with a drop of olive oil. Beat eggs until fluffy and mix in spinach. Add the sweet potatoes to the skillet first and then cover with the spinach/egg mixture. Cook covered over low heat for about 10 minutes, or until a toothpick inserted in the center comes out clean. Cut into slices and serve with salt and pepper as needed.

Chia Seed Pudding

Ingredients

2/3 cup water

1/4 cup chia seeds

Directions

Mix the two ingredients together and stir for several minutes. Place the dish in the refrigerator until it has the consistency of pudding, about 10-15 minutes. Mix in your choice of toppings such as fresh fruit, shredded coconut, nuts, or granola.

Breakfast Pizza

Ingredients

6 beaten eggs

1/4 tsp each salt and pepper

Grated mozzarella cheese

Pizza sauce

2 cups sautéed mushrooms, peppers, onions, or other veggies of your choice

1 cup cooked and chopped ham, bacon, and/or sausage

Directions

Preheat oven to 350°. Mix the beaten eggs with pepper and salt and pour into a lightly greased pie plate. Bake until the eggs are firmly set, about 15 minutes. Remove from oven and spread with pizza sauce, choice of toppings, and grated cheese. Put back in the oven until the cheese is melted and lightly browned, about 5-8 minutes.

Egg And Ham Cups

Ingredients

8 eggs

8 deli ham slices

1 thinly sliced green onion

4 tbsp shredded cheddar cheese

Pepper to taste

Directions

Preheat oven to 400°. Lightly spray 8 muffin cups with cooking spray. Fold each piece of ham in half and line the bottom of each cup with 1 slice. Sprinkle about 1/4 tbsp of green onion and 1/2 tbsp of shredded cheese on top of the ham. Place a raw egg in each cup and sprinkle with pepper. Cook until eggs are as firm as desired, or about 15 minutes.

Breakfast Burritos

Ingredients

2 tortillas (I prefer whole wheat)

2 egg whites

1/4 cup canned beans (like kidney beans, black beans, or pinto beans), rinsed and drained

1/4 cup shredded cheese (sharp cheddar, pepper jack, or Swiss are good choices)

Salsa

Directions

Scrambled egg whites over medium heat in a skillet. Placed half of the scrambled eggs in each tortilla. Sprinkle on with shredded cheese and layer the beans on top. Roll up each tortilla and put in the microwave for about 1 minute. Spoon salsa on top if desired.

Scrambled Eggs With Feta Cheese, Asparagus, And Smoked Salmon

Ingredients

8 eggs

4 ounces of chopped smoked salmon

8 chopped asparagus stalks (remove the woody parts from the bottoms)

1/4 cup crumbled feta cheese

2 tbsp milk

1 tbsp butter

Directions

Melt butter in a skillet over medium heat. Once it begins to foam, toss in the asparagus and cook until tender. Whisk together the eggs and milk and then add to the skillet, reducing the heat to low. Stir constantly to keep eggs from sticking and add the feta cheese about a minute before the eggs are cooked to desired firmness. Remove from heat and mix in the smoked salmon.

Oatmeal Express

Ingredients

1 cup milk, no sugar added almond milk, or unsweetened coconut milk

1 cup instant oatmeal

1/2 tsp ginger

1 tsp flaxseeds

1 tbsp almonds, chopped or sliced

2 tsp honey

Vanilla yogurt

Directions

Mix all of the ingredients together except for the yogurt. Place in the microwave for approximately 2-3 minutes. Top with a dollop of yogurt.

Cheddar, Turkey, And Guacamole Breakfast Sandwich

Ingredients

1 tomato slice, thick

1 slice of cheese (Swiss, Cheddar, Mozzarella, etc)

3 ounces shaved deli turkey breast, smoked or regular

1 egg

1 toasted bagel, croissant, English muffin, or 2 slices of whole grain bread

2 tbsp guacamole

Olive oil

Directions

In a skillet over medium heat, fry the egg in hot oil until the yolk is still slightly runny but the white is firmly set, about 4-5 minutes. In the meantime, place turkey that has been topped with cheese in the microwave until the cheese is melted and the turkey is hot, about 1 minute. On the bottom half of the sandwich, place the fresh tomato and the turkey. Put the egg on top and spread the top piece of the sandwich with guacamole.

Chapter 2: Lunch-- Midday Fuel

There is nothing wrong with having a sandwich at your desk when lunchtime rolls around. With thousands of possible filling combinations, you could have sandwiches forever if that is what you wanted to eat daily.

For those who are looking for new taste experiences that are easy to make, take a walk away from the norm with this amazing collection of lunch choices that will have your taste buds cheering. The majority of these recipes can also be made the evening before as dinner and then taken as leftovers. P.S.-- I broke down and included one sandwich recipe!

Simple Crab And Pasta Salad

Ingredients

1 package crabmeat, chopped

2 cups cooked seashell pasta, al dente

1 cup mayonnaise

1 tbsp vinegar

1 tbsp lemon juice

1 green pepper, diced

1 onion, diced

6 radishes, diced

1/2 black or green olives, diced

1/2 celery, diced

1 tomato, diced

2 tbsp total of your choice of spices (garlic, oregano, basil, dill, etc.)

Directions

Whisk together vinegar, spices, lemon juice, and mayonnaise in a large bowl. Add the pasta, tossing until it is well coated. Add the remaining ingredients and mix well. Cover and keep chilled until ready to eat.

Tomato And Mozzarella Salad

Ingredients

1 cup spinach leaves, rinsed and dried

1 large tomato, cubed

1/2 cup mozzarella cheese, cubed

3 tbsp balsamic vinegar

2 tsp olive oil

1 tbsp seeds (pumpkin, sunflower, chia, flax, etc.)

1 garlic clove, pressed

1/4 tsp pepper

Directions

Toss all ingredients together until well mixed.

Pineapple And Grilled Chicken Sandwich

Ingredients

2 boneless, skinless chicken breasts

2 slices of pineapple

2 minced jalapeno slices

2 slices of cheese (cheddar, Swiss, mozzarella)

2 rolls, bagels, or croissants

4 slices red onion

Teriyaki sauce

Directions

Mix chicken and teriyaki sauce in a plastic bag and shake to coat. Marinate for a minimum of 1 hour. Heat up the grill and take the chicken out of the marinade. Grill for 5-6 minutes and flip, covering each breast with a slice of cheese. Remove from grill when the cheese has melted and the chicken is slightly charred and firm when touched; keep warm and set aside. Place the rolls and pineapple on the grill. Cook the pineapple until tender and the roll until toasted. Top bottom slice with chicken, onion, jalapeno, and pineapple.

Apricot Chicken With Beets

Ingredients

Whole chicken

2 beets, peeled and cubed

4 carrots, peeled and sliced

4 lemon wedges

2 tbsp hot water mixed with 1/2 cup sugar-free (of course!) apricot jam

2 tbsp olive oil

Directions

Preheat oven to 450°. Toss vegetables with half of the mixed jam and oil. Roast for about 10 minutes. Add lemon wedges and chicken to pan; return to oven for 20 minutes. Glaze the chicken with the rest of the jam mixture and roast until cooked all the way through, about another 30 minutes.

Garlic Shrimp Stuffed Avocado

Ingredients

1 avocado

2 cups fresh or defrosted shrimp, medium or large

5 cloves garlic, minced

Fresh parsley

Salt and Pepper

Olive oil

Directions

Cut the avocado in half and remove the pit. Remove most of the avocado meat, leaving just enough for the shell to stand firm. Chop up the removed meat and put in a medium size bowl and coarsely mash; set aside.

Place garlic, 3 tbsp of oil, and shrimp in a skillet. Cook until the shrimp are pink over low heat. Add the skillet mixture to the bowl, toss in freshly chopped parsley, salt and pepper to taste; mix well. Spoon half of the mixture into each shell, sprinkle with parsley if desired.

Lamb Burgers And Mint Tzatziki

Ingredients

1 pound ground lamb

1 cup Greek-style yogurt

1/2 English cucumber, chopped into chunks

1/3 cup chives, chopped

1 tbsp minced garlic

1/3 cup fresh mint leaves, roughly chopped

3 tbsp fresh oregano, chopped

2 tsp lemon juice

2 pitas, warmed

Olive oil

Salt and pepper

Directions

Heat grill to hot. Combine cucumber, yogurt, mint, lemon juice, and half of the garlic, oregano, and chives in a small bowl and add salt and pepper to taste. In a large bowl, mix the lamb and remaining spices gently together. Form into 2 burgers.

Drizzle oil on both sides of the burgers. Grill over medium to high heat, flipping occasionally. Insert a meat thermometer and remove burgers done medium at 140° or medium rare at 130°. Place burgers inside the pitas and serve tzatziki on the side.

Shrimp Scampi

Ingredients

1/2 pound fresh or defrosted shrimp

1 green onion, minced

3 garlic cloves, minced

4 tbsp cream

2 tbsp butter

1/4 cup white wine

1 tsp crushed red pepper flakes

Whole wheat pasta (spaghetti, fettuccini, bowties, etc.)

1/4 cup of water reserved from the pasta

Parmesan cheese

Directions

Cook pasta to desired doneness and strain, reserving 1/4 cup of the water in case you find that the sauce becomes too thick. Add green onion, garlic and butter to the empty pasta pot and sauté for about 1 minute. Add the white wine, red pepper flakes, and shrimp. Cook for 4 minutes, turning shrimp after 2 minutes. Add cream for the last 2 minutes. Put pasta back into the pot and toss to coat. Add pasta water if the sauce is too thick for your liking. Serve sprinkled with parmesan cheese.

Quinoa With Figs, Peppers And Squash

Ingredients

2 cups water

1 cup quinoa

1 cup butternut squash, washed, peeled, and cubed

1 sweet red pepper, seeded and diced

1 cup dried figs, chopped

1/2 tbsp white vinegar

3 tbsp olive oil

Directions

Preheat oven to 350°. Cook quinoa in water until desired tenderness is reached and set aside. Mix the remaining ingredients in a baking dish and roast covered until tender, about 25-30 minutes. Mix in the quinoa and season with salt and pepper if desired.

Chapter 3: Dinner--Food For Thought

The perfect end to a long and busy day is being able to relax around the dinner table and play catch-up with the family. What makes it so perfect is having a delicious meal in the oven with only the shortest amount of preparation time.

Dinner is the main meal of the day for most people. It should not only taste fantastic, but it should also be filling, comforting, and nutritionally balanced. After all, it needs to keep you feeling full until it is time for breakfast.

None of these dishes are at all complicated to make, and none take more than an hour. However, they taste so good that the only one who will know that you did not spend all day in the kitchen is you. Impress your friends or loved ones with culinary masterpieces that show off your skillful chef side!

Beef Tenderloin With Mustard And Horseradish Crust

Ingredients

1 whole beef tenderloin, center cut with all of the excess fat trimmed off

1/2 cup - 1 cup dried breadcrumbs

1 pound small new potatoes, washed

2 tbsp prepared horseradish

4 tbsp Dijon mustard

1/4 cup olive oil

2 tbsp dried parsley

2 tsp garlic powder

Directions

Mix together horseradish and Dijon mustard. Mix in breadcrumbs by hand. The mixture should be moist but if it is too dry, add warm water 1 tsp at a time until it is the desired consistency. Place tenderloin on a sheet of plastic wrap and mold the mustard mixture on top. Completely wrap and set in the refrigerator overnight.

Preheat the oven to 375°. Remove the wrapping from the beef tenderloin and set in the middle of your favorite roasting pan. Toss the potatoes in a large bowl with the olive oil. When they are thoroughly coated, sprinkle on the garlic and parsley and toss again. Place the potatoes around the beef tenderloin. Cook until desired doneness. Medium rare on a meat thermometer will show 145°.

Alternately, this can also be done in the slow cooker. There is no need to marinate the tenderloin if this method is chosen. All of the other directions are the same. Cook on low in the slow cooker for 6-8 hours. If you find that the crust is a little bit soggy, transfer the tenderloin to a baking sheet and put under the broiler at 550° for 5-10 minutes.

Allow tenderloin to sit covered on a cutting board for about 10 minutes before slicing.

Feta And Spinach Stuffed Turkey Breast

Ingredients

1 turkey breast half, 2 pounds boneless

1 package baby spinach leaves, washed and dried

1 cup feta cheese, crumbled

1/2 cup green onions, finely chopped and divided

1 tbsp dried breadcrumbs

4 tbsp water (approximately) divided

1 clove of garlic, minced

2 tbsp olive oil, divided

1 egg white, beaten lightly

3/4 cup white wine (non-alcoholic is fine if you prefer), dry

1/2 tsp oregano

1 cup chicken broth, low sodium

1/2 tsp black pepper

1 tbsp butter

2 tbsp cornstarch

Directions

Over medium- high heat, warm a large saucepan. Add the spinach leaves and 1 tbsp of the water. Cook covered for about 5 minutes, stirring often, until spinach is wilted. Strain in a colander until spinach in no longer moist.

Over medium- high heat, place 1 tbsp of the olive oil, 3 tbsp of the green onions, garlic, and 2 more tbsp of the water. Cover and cook until the moisture has evaporated, about 3 minutes. Transfer mixture into a medium size bowl and add in the breadcrumbs, feta, oregano, 1/4 tsp black pepper, egg white, and spinach. Mix thoroughly.

Place the turkey breast on a cutting surface. Slice through the center horizontally, cutting to, not all the way through, the other side and open as if it were a book. Put the turkey between 2 pieces of plastic wrap and pound evenly to about 1/2 inch thick with a rolling pin or meat mallet. Remove the wrap.

Evenly spread the spinach and feta mixture over the turkey breast, leaving a border of about 1 inch. Starting with one of the short sides, roll up the breast as if it were a jelly roll. Use cooking twine to secure the breast every 2 inches. Rub the remaining 1/4 tsp of black pepper over the breast evenly.

Preheat the oven to 325°. Heat the remaining olive oil over medium heat in a heavy saucepan. Add the turkey breast and cook, turning until all sides are brown, about 8 minutes. Take turkey out of the saucepan and place in a roasting pan. Put the remaining green onions in the saucepan and sauté for about 1 minute. Stir in the white wine and scrape the bottom of the pan to loosen the bits of browned turkey.

Pour the broth into the roaster with the turkey. Bake covered for about 45 minutes, or until a meat thermometer inserted into the thickest portion reaches 170°. Remove turkey breast and wrap with foil to keep warm.

Place the roasting pan over high heat on the top of the stove. Mix the last 1 tbsp of water with the cornstarch and add to the pan, whisking constantly until it comes to a boil. Cook until slightly thickened, about 3 minutes and remove from heat. Stir in the butter. Take the cooking twine off of the turkey breast and slice into portions. Ladle the sauce over the top of each slice and serve.

Tuna Steaks With Lime Sauce And Avocado

Ingredients

4 yellowfin tuna blocks (often also called ahi), sushi quality

2 avocados, peeled, halved, pitted, and sliced

1/2 cup tamari or soy sauce

1 tsp cayenne pepper

4 cloves of garlic, minced

2 tbsp fresh ginger, peeled and minced

1/4 cup cilantro leaves

6 tbsp lime juice, freshly squeezed

1-2 jalapeno peppers, (depending on how much heat you like), seeded and minced

1/2 cup olive oil

2 tbsp canola oil or olive oil

Directions

Mix together the lime juice, soy or tamari sauce, olive oil, garlic, jalapeno peppers, cilantro leaves, and ginger in a small bowl. If a smoother sauce is desired, use a blender to puree.

Heat a large, heavy skilled for one minute on high heat. Coat the skillet with the 2 tbsp of canola or olive oil and allow to heat for just less than a minute. Place the tuna blocks in the skillet, season each with 1/4 tsp cayenne pepper and sear on both sides for one minute apiece.

Remove the tuna and put into a shallow bowl. Gently coat both sides with some of the lime sauce. Pour the remaining sauce evenly over the bottom of four dinner plates and place one piece of the tuna on each. Place a lime wedge on top of each piece and serve the sliced avocado on the side of the plate.

Mexican Style Meatloaf

Ingredients

1 pound extra-lean ground beef

1 egg, slightly beaten

1 tbsp garlic powder

1 cup of salsa (mild, medium, or hot)

2 jalapeno peppers, seeded and diced

1 red onion, diced

1 cup shredded cheddar cheese

Directions

Preheat oven to 350°.

In a large bowl, mix together the ground beef, garlic powder, egg, 1/2 cup of the salsa, 1/2 cup of the shredded cheese, jalapeno peppers, and the onion. Combine thoroughly. Press the meat mixture into a loaf pan lightly sprayed with cooking oil. Pour the remaining salsa on top. Bake for about 45 minutes, or until a toothpick inserted into the center comes out clean. Sprinkle with the other 1/2 cup of shredded cheese and bake for 5 more minutes. Slice and serve with mashed potatoes and extra salsa on the side if desired.

Greek Chicken Spaghetti

Ingredients

4 boneless, skinless, chicken breasts

Spaghetti or other pasta of your choice

4 sweet peppers (I use one each of red, green, yellow, and orange)

2 jars of sliced green olives

4 cloves of garlic, minced

3 cups of crumbled feta cheese

1/2 cup of parmesan cheese

1/2 cup olive oil

Directions

Cook chicken breasts with a dash of olive oil in a skillet over medium- high heat, about 6-7 minutes per side. Remove to a cutting board and slice into bite size strips or cubes. Return to skillet over medium heat and add olives, peppers, garlic, and olive oil. Simmer covered until vegetables are tender, about 10 minutes. Meanwhile, cook your choice of pasta and drain.

Add the feta cheese and cook until slightly melted, about 5 minutes. Remove from heat and stir in parmesan cheese. Pour into pasta and toss.

Cajun Scallops

Ingredients

1 tbsp Cajun seasoning, or to taste

1 tbsp olive oil

1 tsp butter

1 tsp black pepper

1 red onion, diced

1 clove of garlic, minced

2 tbsp hot sauce of your choice (Tabasco or Frank's work well)

1 pound of fresh scallops, rinsed and drained

Directions

Using a heavy skillet, heat the olive oil over high heat for about 1 minute. Add the Cajun seasoning, red onion, and black pepper. Sauté for 3-4 minutes. Add in the garlic and the butter. Sauté for another minute. Toss in the scallops and cook until lightly browned, about 1-2 minutes. Turn scallops and liberally apply the hot sauce. Cook until done, about 4-5 minutes.

Sausage And Peppers

Ingredients

8-10 mild or hot Italian sausages (these are much easier to slice after they have been cooked)

3 green peppers, seeded and sliced

2 red peppers, seeded and sliced

2 large red onions, cut into chunky slices

3 stalks of celery, cut diagonally

2 cups of whole grain rice

Directions

Cook the Italian sausages in a skillet over medium heat, turning so that all sides are evenly browned. Pierce each one with a sharp knife several times and allow the juice to flow into the skillet. Remove the sausages to a cutting board and slice into bite-sized chunks.

Place the red peppers, green peppers, onions, and celery in the skillet and sauté in the sausage drippings until celery is tender, about 8-10 minutes. Put the sausage back in the skillet while you prepare the rice according to the package directions. If you are a lover of all things spicy, now is a good time to use a free hand with the hot sauce bottle if you like. Cooking the hot sauce releases even more heat.

Place the rice on each plate and make a small hollow area. Ladle the sausage and peppers into the hole.

Tangy Buffalo Chicken Pizza

Ingredients

1 whole deli roasted chicken, chopped into small chunks

3/4 cup any brand hot sauce, Buffalo-style

1/2 cup blue cheese, crumbled

1 1/2 cups shredded pizza mozzarella cheese

1 lime

1 store bought whole wheat pizza crust (any brand will do just fine)

Directions

Evenly spread the hot sauce around the crust. Place the chicken on top of the hot sauce and cover with the mozzarella cheese. Sprinkle the blue cheese on top of the mozzarella. Bake according to the directions on the pizza crust and remove from the oven when the cheese is golden brown and bubbling. Squeeze the lime over each slice just before serving.

Pork Tenderloin Medallions In Red Wine And Mushroom Sauce

Ingredients

1 whole pork tenderloin, sliced into about 1 inch thick, round medallions

1 cup of low sodium beef broth

2 cups of red wine (non-alcoholic if you prefer), dry

1 cup of cream

2 packages of fresh sliced mushrooms, washed, rinsed, and drained

1 cup of water

2 tbsp fresh parsley, coarsely chopped

1 large Spanish onion, diced

1 package of egg noodles (or any other type of pasta)

2 tbsp olive oil

Directions

Heat the oil in a large skillet over medium-high heat. Add the tenderloin medallions and brown on each side. Remove from the skillet and cover with foil. Combine the water, beef broth, red wine, onion, and mushrooms to the skillet. Cover and simmer for about 20 minutes over medium heat, stirring occasionally. Mix in the cream and parsley.

Return the tenderloin back into the skillet and bring back to a covered simmer. Reduce heat to low and prepare your choice of pasta. When the pasta is cooked to the desired tenderness, allow to drain and put onto plates.

Place the tenderloin medallions on top of the pasta and cover with the mushroom sauce.

Bonus Recipe: Cheesy Beef And Beet Crock Pot Chili

Ingredients

4 cans of kidney beans, rinsed and drained

2 cans of sliced mushroom, including juice

2 cans of diced tomatoes, including juice

2 pounds of beets, washed, peeled, and cubed

1 head of celery, washed and chopped

2 large Spanish onions, peeled and chopped

3 cups of shredded cheddar cheese

3 cups of water

1/2 cup chili powder or to taste

2-3 pounds fresh, extra-lean ground beef

Directions

Combine kidney beans, mushrooms, diced tomatoes, beets, celery, onions, water, chili powder, and 1 cup of the cheese in a crock pot set on low. Crumble in the ground beef and mix well. Cover and allow to cook all day, or at least for 6-8 hours.

About half an hour before the chili is ready to dish out, check to be certain that the beets are tender. If not, turn the crock pot up to high. Just before serving, mix in the remaining 2 cups of shredded cheese and stir until melted. Top each bowl with a dollop of sour cream if desired.

NOTE*

For the recipes that call for wine, if you are using the with alcohol versions, it should be noted that alcohol evaporates during cooking. By adding the wine at the beginning, instead of near the end, the dishes retain all of the flavor of the wine but almost none of the alcohol content.

Chapter 4: Bonus Dessert Recipes

What would a meal be without the dessert to finish it off? Just because it is dessert, that does not mean that it has to be loaded with sugar and empty calories. Try these satisfying and comforting taste sensations!

No Sugar Pumpkin Pie

Ingredients

1 prebaked pie shell

2 cups canned pure pumpkin (not pumpkin pie filling)

2 cups skim or 1% milk

2 small boxes of vanilla flavored instant pudding, sugar free

1 tsp cinnamon

1/2 tsp nutmeg

1/4 tsp ginger

Directions

Place all of the ingredients in a blender and blend on low until combined. Increase speed to high and blend until smooth. Pour into the pie shell and cover with plastic wrap to prevent a skin from forming. Chill until set, usually about 4 hours.

Berry Burst Flan Tart

Ingredients

1 sugar free flan tart (in the bakery section of your local supermarket)

1 bag frozen mixed berries and any other fruits you choose, no sugar added, defrosted with juice

1/4 cup honey

Directions

Mix the honey with the defrosted fruits and juice in a saucepan over low heat. Gently warm but do not allow to boil. Remove from heat and let stand for about 5 minutes so that it thickens slightly. Spoon the mixture over each piece of flan tart, drizzling juice over top. Serve with sugar free vanilla yogurt if desired.

Cinnamon Vanilla Mousse

Ingredients

2 packages sugar free vanilla instant pudding mix

2 cups heavy whipping cream

1 tbsp cinnamon

Directions

In a medium size bowl, pour in the whipping cream. Using a hand mixer on medium, whip just until the cream begins to thicken. Add in the vanilla pudding mix and the cinnamon. Continue whipping until blended. Increase speed to high until light and fluffy. Spoon into dishes and sprinkle with cinnamon.

No Bake Pumpkin Cheesecake

This cheesecake definitely takes your mind off the fact that there is no added sugar and leaves you satisfied.
Preparation time: 1 hours 10 minutes
Yield: 6 servings
Ingredients:

- Pumpkin Puree (1 can)
- Cream Cheese (8 oz., cold)
- Pudding mix (1 package of instant sugar free, vanilla flavored)
- Skim milk (½ cup)
- Whipped topping (1 container of frozen fat-free)
- Pumpkin pie spice (1 tsp.)

Directions:
1. Add the first three ingredients in an electric mixer and mix on medium until combined.

2. Add your milk, half your whipping cream and your pumpkin spice then continue to mix.

3. Pour your mixture into an 8-inch pie plate, and top with the other half of the whipping topping.

4. Let it chill for at least 1 hour in the refrigerator. 5. Serve and enjoy!

No Bake Cherry Pie

This cream filled cherry pie brings you to heaven with every slice.
Preparation time: 1 hours 10 minutes
Yield: 8 servings
Ingredients:

- Graham cracker crust (9-inches, prepared)
- Milk (1 cup, cold)
- Pudding mix (1 package of instant sugar free, vanilla flavored)
- Whipped topping (1 container of frozen fat-free)
- Cherries (1 can, crushed and drained)

Directions:
1. Add all the ingredients except the crust in a medium bowl and mix.
2. Pour the mixture into the prepared crust.
3. Let it chill for at least an hour in a refrigerator.
4. Serve and enjoy!

Pineapple Milkshake

This sweet and tasty drink is a brilliant end to a heavy meal.
Preparation time: 20 minutes
Yield: 1 serving
Ingredients:

- Frozen pineapple (3 cups)
- Greek yogurt (1 cup, pineapple/vanilla flavored)
- Unsweetened vanilla almond milk (1 cup)
- Vanilla extract (1 tbs.)

Directions:
1. Add the ingredients in the blender and blend until smooth. 2. Serve and enjoy!

Melon Sorbet

This dessert is a refreshing and sweet way to end your meal.
Preparation time: 5 minutes
Yield: 6 servings
Ingredients:

- 4½ cups ice cubes, crushed
- ½ lb. Melon, cubed
- 1 tbsp. grated orange zest
- 2 tbsp. honey

Directions:
1. Place all ingredients in a blender.
2. Blend the ingredients for 30 seconds.
3. Serve immediately. NB: We suggest that you make the sorbet in batches.

Raspberry Icy Pops

These desserts are always a hit with the kids.
Preparation time: 4 hours 30 minutes
Yield: 8 servings
Ingredients:

- Boiling water (1 cup)
- Jell-O (1 package, raspberry)
- Raspberries (1 cup, fresh)
- Plain yogurt (1 cup)

Directions:
1. Add all the ingredients in a blender. Blend everything thing until it is smooth. 2. Put mixture into a popsicle mold and place to freeze until frozen.

Chocolate Coated Strawberry

This delight is simply made with strawberries coated in chocolate.
Preparation time: 15 minutes
Yield: 10 servings
Ingredients

- 1 cup raw chocolate
- 10–12 fresh strawberries
- 1 tbsp. butter
- ¼ cup chocolate syrup

Directions
1. Melt the chocolate with chocolate syrup add butter, leave to cool.
2. Now dip halved strawberry into chocolate mixture and place on platter.
3. Repeat the same procedure for all strawberries.
4. Place the platter into the freezer for 25 minutes.
5. Serve and enjoy.

Pecan Pie

Here is a delicious sugar free recipe for the classic pecan pie.

Preparation time: 2 hours 10 minutes
Yield: 8 servings
Ingredients:

- Graham cracker crust (9-inches, prepared)
- Milk (1 cup, cold)
- Pudding mix (1 package of instant sugar free, vanilla flavored)
- Whipped topping (1 container of frozen fat-free)
- Pecan (1 cup, crushed)

Directions:
1. Set your crust aside then mix all your remaining ingredients in a medium bowl.
2. Pour the mixture into the prepared crust.
3. Let it chill for an hour in a refrigerator.

Apple Muffins

If you are a fan of apples, and soft pastry then you will love these muffins.

Preparation time: 35 minutes
Yield: 12 muffins
Ingredients:

- 1 cup cooked and cubed apples
- 2 teaspoons baking soda
- tbsp. milk
- 1 tsp. allspice
- 1 tsp. cinnamon
- 1¾ cups all-purpose flour
- 2 eggs
- 1 tbsp. vegetable oil
- ¾ cup honey
- ½ cup chocolate chips, chopped

1. Preheat oven to 350°F and line 12-hole muffin tin with paper cases.
2. In a bowl combine the flour, cinnamon, allspice, and

baking soda.
3. In a blender process the apples, milk, oil, eggs, and honey until smooth.
4. Fold the apple mix into the dry ingredients and stir until just combined. Stir in the chocolate chips and spoon the batter into paper cases to ⅔ full.
5. Bake the muffins for 25 minutes or until firm to the touch. Remove from the oven and allow cooling for 10 minutes. Remove from the tin and serve.

Peanut Cookies

Now you can enjoy delicious cookies with the added refined sugar.
Preparation time: 25 minutes
Yield: 24 cookies
Ingredients:

- ½ cup honey
- 1 egg
- ¾ cup whole-wheat flour
- ½ cup crushed peanuts
- ½ teaspoon almond extract
- ½ cup butter spread
- 1 tbsp. milk
- ¼ teaspoon baking soda

1. Preheat oven to 350°F and line baking sheet with baking paper.
2. In a blender, combine the butter spread, egg, honey, almond extract, and milk. Process until smooth.
3. Add the baking soda, peanuts, and flours. Process for 15 seconds more or until blended thoroughly.

4. Drop the cookie batter onto cookie sheet and bake for 15 minutes. 5. Cool, serve and enjoy.

Coffee Cheesecake

Who doesn't love a delicious slice of coffee cheesecake? Now you can enjoy a slice of heaven without the residual guilt.

Preparation time: 2 hours 30 minutes
Yield: 12 servings
Ingredients:

- Graham cracker crumbs (1½ cups)
- Pecans (1½ cups)
- Butter (4 tbs.)
- Cream cheese (3 packages, softened)
- Honey (1 cup)
- Eggs (3)
- Vanilla extract (1 tsp.)
- Instant espresso coffee powder (4 tsp.)
- All-purpose flour (2 tbs.)
- Sour cream (1 cup)

Directions:

1. Preheat the oven 400°F. Press the crumbs into the bottom and ½ up the sides of one 9-inch springform pan.
2. Beat the cream cheese and the honey until it is fluffy in a large bowl. Add the rest of the ingredients and mix until smooth.
3. Pour the mixture into the prepared crust.
4. Put the pie in the oven for 15 minutes then reduced the heat to 300°F and cooked for 30 minutes or until the cheese set but jiggles somewhat in the center. Let the cake cool for 2 hours.

5. Put the cake in the fridge for 3 hours. 6. Serve and enjoy!

Strawberry Sorbet

The taste of strawberry is great, but strawberry sorbet is splendid.

Preparation time: 2 hours 30 minutes
Yield: 4 servings
Ingredients:

- Water (1 cup)
- Splenda granular (1 cup)
- Strawberries (5 cups)
- Lemon juice (¼ cup)

1. Add water and Splenda in a large cup. Ensure that the Splenda is dissolved in the water.
2. Put the berries in a blender and puree until smooth. Add the Splenda mix in the blender as well pulse till everything is combined.
3. Pour the mixture into an ice cream machine and freeze until thick. 4. Serve and enjoy!

Walnut Cookies

Here is a sugar free recipe that the whole family will love.

Preparation time: 30 minutes
Yield: 24 cookies
Ingredients:

- All-purpose flour (1¼ cups)
- Baking powder (1 tsp.)
- Baking soda (¼ tsp.)
- Salt (¼ tsp.)
- Butter (½ cup)
- Honey (¼ cup)
- Eggs (1, lightly beaten)
- Pecans (1 cup, chopped)
- Vanilla extract (½ tsp.)

1. Preheat the oven to 375°F. Sift the first four ingredients together.
2. Mix the butter and the honey until it has a creamy texture in a large bowl. Add the rest of the ingredients

and mix until combined.
3. Make your cookie shape and put it on an ungreased baking sheet.
4. Put it in the oven for 10 minutes then let it cool afterward. 5. Serve and enjoy!

Chocolate Maca Blast

This amazing treat is made from pure cocoa infused with the flavors of tropical fruit and maca (an ingredient made famous by Peru). It's simple, quick to make and best of all delicious.

Preparation time: 5 minutes
Yield: 1 serving

Ingredients

- Spinach (1 Cup)
- Banana (½, frozen)
- Mango (½ cup)
- Maca Powder (1 tsp.)
- Cacao (1 tbsp.)
- Cacao Nibs (1 tbsp.)
- Almond Butter (1 tbsp.)
- Ceylon Cinnamon (½ tsp.)
- Almond Milk (1½ cups)

Directions

1. Add all your ingredients into a blender.

2. Pulse for until smooth (should take about 20 seconds). 3. Enjoy!

Blueberry Cacao Blast

Simple yet delicious dessert smoothie.
Preparation time: 5 minutes
Yield: 1 serving
Ingredients:

- 1 cup blueberries
- 1 dash honey
- 1 tbsp. raw cacao nibs
- 1 tbsp. chia seeds
- 1 dash cinnamon
- ½ Spinach (chopped)
- ½ Cup Bananas (chopped)
- 1½ Cup Almond milk

Directions:
1. Place raspberries, cacao nibs, chia seeds, and cinnamon in a blender.
2. Add enough almond milk to reach the max line.
3. Process for 30 seconds or until you get a smooth mixture.
4. Serve immediately in the chilled tall glass.

Raw Fudge

We all love fudge, and now we bring you the simplest version you can find. It requires minimum effort and time to prepare.

Preparation time: 10 minutes + inactive time
Yield: 6 servings
Ingredients:

- 1 tbsp. coconut butter
- ¾ cup walnuts
- 2 dates, pitted
- ⅓ cup cacao powder
- 3 tbsp. coconut oil
- ¾ cup pecan nuts

Directions:
1. Add all ingredient to a blender.
2. Process until you have a thick consistency.
3. Line a baking dish with parchment paper and spread

the prepared mix in the prepared dish. 4. Cover with foil and refrigerate for 2 hours. 5. Slice and serve.

Blueberry Enchanting Muffins

Make these muffins and serve with tea.
Preparation time: 45 minutes
Yield: 6 servings
Ingredients

- 2 cups all-purpose flour
- ½ tsp. baking powder
- 1 pinch salt
- 3 tbsp. oil
- ½ cup milk
- 1 cup blueberries
- ½ cup honey

Directions
1. In a bowl, add flour, salt, oil, milk, baking powder, and honey, then mix well.
2. Fold in blueberries.
3. Pour this batter into greased muffin cups.
4. Bake for 30–35 minutes. 5. Serve and enjoy.

Coconut Dates Balls

This sugarless delight will blow your mind.
Preparation time: 25 minutes
Yield: 6 servings

Ingredients

- ½ cup ripe dates seeded
- ½ cup honey
- 2 tbsp. butter, melted
- 1 cup cocoa powder
- 1 cup coconut, shredded
- ½ cup milk

Direction
1. In a blender add all ingredients and blend well.
2. Now make small round balls.
3. Transfer to a platter and place in freezer for 30 minutes.
4. Serve and enjoy.

Strawberry Truffles

Your family members will surely love this dessert.

Preparation time: 45 minutes
Yield: 8 servings

Ingredients

- 1 cup cream
- 1 cup raw chocolate, melted
- 1 teaspoon vanilla extract
- ¼ cup honey
- 2 tbsp. butter, melted
- 1 cup strawberry puree
- ½ cup coconut powder

Directions

1. In a saucepan add cream, coconut powder, strawberry puree, honey, butter, and stir continuously. Cook for 10–15 minutes.
2. Add vanilla extract and stir.
3. Transfer to the freezer for 30 minutes.
4. Now scope out small round balls and place into the

platter.
5. Transfer to the freezer for 10 minutes.
6. Dip into melted chocolate and place again into freezer for 10 minutes. 7. Serve and enjoy.

Chocolate And Banana Pudding

Make this pudding and place in the fridge for better results.

Preparation time: 120 minutes
Yield: 5 servings

Ingredients

- 1 cup milk
- 1 cup chocolate, melted
- 4 bananas, peeled, sliced
- ½ cup condensed milk
- ½ cup honey
- 2 tbsp. butter
- 2 tbsp. cocoa powder
- 1 cup whipped cream

Directions

1. In a sauce pan add butter with and leave to cook until reduced to half.
2. Now add condensed milk, chocolate, honey, cocoa

powder, and stir gradually.
3. Pour half of chocolate pudding into a large dish and place banana slices evenly.
4. Pour remaining chocolate on top and freeze for 2 hours.
5. Top with whipped cream before serving. 6. Enjoy.

Cheery Cheesecake

This dessert is highly delicious.
Preparation time: 120 minutes
Yield: 4 servings
Ingredients

- 2 cups cherries
- 1 cup honey
- 2 tbsp. lemon juice
- 3 cups cream cheese
- 1 cup whipped cream
- 1 cup cherries
- ½ cup caster sugar
- 2 tbsp. butter, melted
- 2 packages graham crackers, crumbled
- 1 cup condense milk
- ½ cup caster sugar

Directions
1. Beat cream cheese and honey until fluffy.
2. Now add condensed milk, caster sugar, and wiped

cream, fold well.
3. In a saucepan add cherries, lemon juice, and sugar, stir continually till sugar is dissolved. Let it cool well.
4. Spread crumbled crackers into the dish and pour melted butter. Press with a spoon.
5. Transfer cheese mixture and spread well.
6. Place it into the freezer for 4 hours. 7. Top with cooked cherries while serving.

Blackberry Cheesecake

Try this delight and make your friend and family happy.
Preparation time: 30 minutes
Yield: 4 servings
Ingredients

- 1 cup blackberry puree
- 1 teaspoon vanilla extract
- 3 cups cream cheese
- ½ cup whipped cream
- 1 cup blackberries
- 1 cup honey
- 2 tbsp. butter, melted
- 3 egg whites
- 1 cup condense milk
- 2 packages of graham crackers, crumbled

Directions
1. Preheat oven to 350°F.
2. Beat egg whites till fluffy.
3. In separate bowl beat cream cheese until fuzzy.
4. Now add in it whipped cream, whipped egg whites,

blackberry puree, honey, butter, condensed milk, vanilla and fold it.
5. Spread crumbled crackers into greased round baking pan and press well.
6. Pour cheese mixture and set it with a spatula evenly.
7. Bake for 25–30 minutes.
8. When the cake is made, place it into the freezer for 20 minutes. 9. Top with blackberries and serve.

Coconut Cheesecake

This cheesecake is extremely enchanting.
Preparation time: 35 minutes
Yield: 5 servings
Ingredients

- ½ cup corn starch
- 1 teaspoon vanilla extract
- 5 oz. cream cheese
- 1 cup milk powder
- 2 tbsp. coconut powder
- 3 tbsp. lemon juice
- 5 tbsp. butter, melted
- 3 egg whites
- ½ cup heavy cream
- 1 cup honey
- 1 package graham crackers, crumbled

1. Preheat oven to 350°F.
2. Beat egg whites till fluffy.
3. Add cream cheese and beat again for 10 minutes.

4. Now in a bowl add coconut powder, vanilla, cream, lemon juice, milk powder, honey and beat well.
5. Combine it with eggs mixture and fold slightly.
6. Spread crumbled graham crackers into greased baking pan and poured melted butter, press with a spoon.
7. Pour cheese mixture and bake for 25–30 minutes.
8. Let to cool and then top with crushed coconut. 9. Enjoy.

Honey And Lemon Cake

This cheesecake is tremendously yummy.
Preparation time: 40 minutes
Yield: 4 servings

Ingredients

- 2 cups all-purpose flour
- 2 tbsp. lemon zest
- 2 tbsp. lemon juice
- 1 teaspoon baking powder
- ¼ teaspoon baking soda
- ½ cup butter
- 1 pinch salt
- 4 eggs
- 1 cup coconut milk
- 1½ cup honey
- ½ cup apple jam, sugar free

1. Preheat oven to 350°F.
2. Combine flour, salt, baking powder, baking soda, eggs, lemon juice, butter, milk, 1 tbsp. lemon zest and beat with electric beater.

3. Transfer to greased baking pan and bake for 30 minutes.
4. Combine apple jam with honey.
5. Pour this mixture over cake and top with lemon zest. 6. Serve and enjoy.

Strawberry Cake

This sweet course is exceedingly enjoyable.
Preparation time: 50 minutes
Yield: 6 servings

Ingredients

- 2 cups all-purpose flour
- 1 cup fresh strawberries
- 2 cup strawberry puree
- 1 tsp. baking powder
- 1 cup butter
- 1 pinch salt
- 2 eggs
- 1 cup milk
- 1 cup honey
- 1 cup whipped cream
- 1 tsp. vanilla extract

Directions
1. Preheat oven to 350°F.
2. In a bowl add flour, eggs, honey, salt, baking powder, milk, butter, vanilla extract, and beat well.
3. Add strawberry puree and stir.
4. Pour into greased cake pan and bake for 30 minutes.
5. Toss caster sugar with whipped cream to combine.
6. Once the cake has cooled, top it with whipped cream and place strawberries.

Creamy Carrot Cake

This unique recipe is very easy to make and delicious too.

Preparation time: 120 minutes
Yield: 4 servings

Ingredients

- 2 cups all-purpose flour
- 1 cup mango chunks
- 2 carrots, shredded
- 1 tsp. baking powder
- ¼ tsp. baking soda
- 1 tsp. vanilla extract
- 1 cup butter
- 1 pinch salt
- 3 eggs
- 1 cup milk
- 1 cup honey
- 1 cup whipped cream

Directions
1. Preheat oven to 350°F.
2. Beat eggs, butter, honey, sifted flour, baking powder, baking soda, salt, vanilla extract, and milk.
3. Add in mango chunks and carrots, fold with a spatula.
4. Pour this mixture into greased round cake mold and bake for 30 minutes.
5. Cut the cake into 3 equal layers when cooled.
6. Combine caster sugar with whipped cream.
7. Add 5–6 tbsp. of whipped cream and spread well.

8. Top with the second layer of cake and spread cream on it. Repeat the same process with the third layer.

Raspberry Pie

This pie is made with a hot taste of ginger.

Preparation time: 40 minutes

Yield: 6 servings

Ingredients

- 2 unbaked pie crusts
- 1 egg, whisked
- 1 cup raspberries
- ½ cup strawberries
- 1 cup honey
- 2 tbsp. brown sugar
- 2 tbsp. lime juice
- 1-inch ginger sliced

Directions

1. Preheat oven to 350°F.

2. In a saucepan add honey, strawberries, raspberries, lime juice, ginger slice, and leave to cook until smooth.

Stir continuously.

3. Discard the ginger slice.

4. Spread one pie sheet into a baking dish and top with raspberry mixture. Place another pie sheet on top and brush with egg and dust sugar.
5. Bake for 20 minutes or until golden brown. 6. Serve and enjoy.

Pineapple Pie

This is a traditional pie recipe.
Preparation time: 30 minutes
Yield: 8 servings
Ingredients

- 2 eggs
- 2 cups pineapple chunks
- 4 tbsp. butter
- ½ teaspoon baking powder
- 1 cup all-purpose flour
- 2 tbsp. honey
- 2 tbsp. vinegar
- ½ cup milk

Directions
1. Preheat oven to 350°F.
2. In a bowl, add one egg and whisk well.
3. Add in flour, honey, butter, and baking powder, mix well.
4. Pour milk and knead a soft dough.

5. In a bowl, add pineapple chunks and vinegar, toss to combine.
6. Transfer into a round baking dish and top with rolled out the dough. Trim the excess sides.
7. Crack an egg in a bowl and brush it on the crust.
8. Bake for 25 minutes. 9. Enjoy.

Almond Cookies

Almond cookies are unique and enjoyable.
Preparation time: 40 minutes
Yield: 6 servings

Ingredients

- 2 cups wheat flour
- 1 cup coconut milk
- ½ teaspoon baking powder
- 4 tbsp. butter
- 2 eggs
- 1 cup caster sugar
- ¼ cup honey
- ½ cup almonds, chopped

Directions
1. Preheat oven to 350°F.
2. In a bowl, add all ingredients and knead a soft dough.
3. Make circular biscuits with dough.

4. Place into the greased baking tray. Bake for 30 minutes. 5. Serve and enjoy.

Lemon Cupcakes

Lemon cupcakes will blow your mind.

Preparation time: 40 minutes
Yield: 5 servings

Ingredients

- 2 cups all-purpose flour
- 1 tbsp. lemon zest
- ½ teaspoon baking powder
- 1 pinch baking soda
- 4 tbsp. butter
- 2 eggs
- ½ cup heavy cream
- 1 cup honey
- 1 cup sour cream

Directions
1. Preheat oven to 350°F.
2. Beat eggs till fluffy.
3. Add butter and honey, beat again for 1–2 minutes.

4. Add flour, lemon zest, baking powder, baking soda, cream, and stir gradually.
5. Pour this batter into greased cups.
6. Bake for 30–35 minutes or until golden brown.
7. Fill a piping bag with sour cream and pipe over cupcakes. 8. Sprinkle some lemon zest on top.

Strawberry Velvet Cupcake

Your kids will be happy with these cakes.
Preparation time: 40 minutes
Yield: 4 servings

Ingredients

- 1 cups all-purpose flour
- ½ cup strawberry puree
- 1 pinches red food color
- ½ teaspoon baking powder
- 3 tbsp. butter
- 2 eggs
- ½ cup milk
- 1 cup honey
- 1 cup whipped cream

Directions
1. Preheat oven to 350°F.
2. Beat eggs till fluffy.
3. Add butter and ½ cup honey, beat again for 1–2

minutes.
4. Add flour, strawberry puree, baking powder, food color, and milk, stir gradually.
5. Pour this batter into greased cups.
6. Bake for 30–35 minutes or until golden brown.
7. Combine remaining honey with whipped cream and add to piping bag. 8. Pipe over the cupcakes and add sprinkles if you like.

Chapter 5: Sugar Free Cake And Pie Recipes

No Bake Strawberry Cheesecake

Ingredients

3/4 cup graham cracker crumbs

3 tablespoons butter, melted

1/4 teaspoon ground cinnamon

1/4 teaspoon ground nutmeg

1 (8 ounce) package cream cheese, softened

1 1/2 cups milk

1 (1 ounce) package cheesecake flavor sugar-free instant pudding mix

2 pints fresh strawberries, sliced

Directions

Mix together graham cracker crumbs, melted butter, cinnamon, and nutmeg in a bowl.

Press the mixture into an 8-inch pie dish. Refrigerate while making filling.

Beat cream cheese in a mixing bowl with an electric mixer on medium speed until softened. reduce the speed to low, and gradually beat in milk, a little at a time (mixture will be watery). Use a rubber spatula to scrape cream cheese from the sides of the bowl, if necessary.

Beat in pudding mix until the filling is thick and smooth. Spoon half of the cream cheese filling into the bottom of the graham cracker crust.

Spread half the strawberries over the filling. Repeat cheesecake layer and strawberry layer.

Chill pie in refrigerator until set and cold, at least 1 hour.

Apple Pie

Ingredients

2 (9 inch) pie shell

3 tablespoons cornstarch

1 tablespoon ground cinnamon

1 (12 fluid ounce) can unsweetened apple juice concentrate, thawed

6 cups sliced green apples

Directions

Preheat oven to 350 degrees F (175 degrees C).

In a small bowl whisk together cornstarch, cinnamon, and 1/3 cup of the apple juice concentrate. Set aside.

In a large saucepan simmer apples with remaining apple juice concentrate until apples are tender, about 10 minutes. Stir in cornstarch mixture and continue to simmer until thickened. Remove from heat.

Spoon apple mixture into pastry-lined pie plate. Cover with top crust. Seal and flute edges. Cut steam vents in top.

Bake in preheated oven for 45 minutes, or until crust is golden brown.

Key Lime Pie

Ingredients

1 cup ground pecans

3 tablespoons butter, melted

2 (1 gram) packets Splenda

1/2 teaspoon coconut extract

1/2 cup heavy cream

2 (1 gram) packets Splenda

1 (.6 ounce) package sugar-free lime-flavor Jello

1/3 cup boiling water

1/3 cup cold water

2 (8 ounce) packages cream cheese, cut into pieces and softened

1/2 teaspoon coconut extract

2 tablespoons ground pecans

Directions

In a medium bowl, mix together 1 cup ground pecans, butter, 2 packets sweetener, and 1/2 teaspoon coconut extract. Press firmly into bottom and up sides of an 8 inch pie plate; refrigerate until firm.

In a small bowl, whip the heavy cream with 2 packets sweetener until soft peaks form. Set aside.

In a large bowl with high sides, mix the gelatin with boiling water until all the gelatin has dissolved.

Then stir in the cold water. With an electric mixer, slowly beat in the cream cheese. After all cream cheese is added, stir in remaining 1/2 teaspoon coconut extract, and beat at high speed until smooth.

Carefully fold in the whipped cream. Use a spatula to scrape mixture into the pie pan and spread around. Sprinkle remaining 2 tablespoons ground nuts on top.

Refrigerate several hours or overnight to allow gelatin to set thoroughly.

Strawberry Pie

Ingredients

24 ounces fresh strawberries

1 (2.1 ounce) package sugar-free cook and serve vanilla pudding mix

1 (.6 ounce) package sugar-free strawberry flavored Jell-O(R)

2 cups water

Directions

Rinse and hull strawberries. Distribute evenly in a 10 inch pie pan.

In a medium saucepan combine pudding mix, gelatin mix, and water. Stir well and bring to a full boil.

Pour mixture over strawberries and refrigerate for 4 to 6 hours. Top with light frozen whipped topping prior to serving, if desired.

Apple Raisin Cake

Ingredients

2 cups all-purpose flour

1 teaspoon baking powder

1 teaspoon baking soda

1/2 teaspoon ground cinnamon

1/2 teaspoon ground nutmeg

1/2 teaspoon salt

1 1/2 cups unsweetened applesauce

3/4 cup brown sugar twin

2 eggs

1 teaspoon vanilla extract

1/2 cup raisins

Directions

Preheat oven to 350 degrees F (175 degrees C). Spray an 8x4 inch loaf pan with cooking spray.

Sift together flour, baking powder, baking soda, cinnamon, nutmeg and salt. Set aside.

Beat the eggs until light and add sugar twin. Add applesauce and vanilla.

Add flour mixture and beat until smooth. Fold in raisins.

Pour batter into loaf pan. Bake at 350F for about an hour, or until a toothpick inserted into cake comes out clean.

Banana Cake

Ingredients

1 cup banana, mashed

1/4 cup butter, softened

1/4 cup water

1/2 cup applesauce, unsweetened

3 large eggs

2 cups whole wheat flour

2 tsp baking powder

1 tsp baking soda

1 tsp cinnamon

1 cup chopped walnuts

Directions

Preheat oven to 350 F or 180 C. Grease and flour a 9 x 13 inch pan.

Beat together mashed banana and soft butter until creamy. Beat in water and applesauce.

In a separate bowl, beat eggs until very foamy. Mix eggs into banana mixture.

In a separate bowl, blend flour, baking powder, baking soda and cinnamon; add to banana mixture and beat until very smooth. Stir in walnuts.

Cook at 350 for 20 minutes or until knife inserted comes out clean.

Moist Chocolate Cake

Ingredients

3/4 cup egg beaters

1 cup skim milk

1/2 cup canola oil

2.25 cup Splenda

2 tsp vanilla extract

1.75 cup white flour

3/4 cup cocoa unsweetened

1.5 tsp baking powder

1.5 tsp baking soda

1 cup water

Directions

Preheat oven to 350F. Grease and flour two 9-inch round cake pans or one 9 x 13-inch oblong baking pan.

Combine eggs, milk, oil and vanilla in a large mixing bowl. Combine dry ingredients - Splenda through baking soda in a large bowl and add to mixture.

Beat with electric mixer at medium speed for two minutes. Stir in boiling water slowly and mix thoroughly.

Add shaved chocolate. Pour into pans. Place in oven and bake for 30-35 minutes or until toothpick inserted in center comes out clean.

Cool in pans for ten minutes then remove from pans to wire cooling rack.

Walnut Brownies

Ingredients

1/2 cup margarine

1/4 cup unsweetened cocoa powder

2 eggs

1 cup granular sucrolose sweetener

3/4 cup all-purpose flour

1/8 teaspoon salt

1/4 cup skim milk

1/2 cup chopped walnuts

1 (1.4 ounce) package sugar free, chocolate fudge flavored instant pudding

1 cup skim milk

Directions

Preheat oven to 350 degrees F (175 degrees C). Grease and flour an 8x8 inch pan.

In a small saucepan over medium heat, melt margarine and cocoa together, stirring occasionally until smooth. Remove from heat and set aside to cool. In a large bowl, beat eggs until frothy. Stir in the sucrolose sweetener.

Combine the flour and salt; stir into the egg mixture then mix in the cocoa and margarine. Finally stir in the 1/4 cup of milk and if desired, the walnuts. Pour into the prepared pan.

Bake for 25 to 30 minutes in the preheated oven, until a toothpick inserted into the center, comes out clean. To make frosting, Mix together the sugar free chocolate pudding mix and 1 cup skim milk using an electric mixer.

Mix for about two minutes or until thick. Spread over cooled brownies before cutting into squares.

Blueberry Coffee Cake

Ingredients

3/4 cup butter, melted and cooled

1 cup milk

3 eggs

1 teaspoon vanilla extract

1 1/2 cups granular sucrolose sweetener

2 teaspoons baking powder

3 cups all-purpose flour

1 3/4 cups fresh or frozen blueberries

1 1/2 cups malitol brown sugar substitute

3/4 cup flour

2 teaspoons ground cinnamon

1/2 cup butter, softened

Directions

Preheat the oven to 350 degrees F (175 degrees C). Grease and flour a 9x13 inch baking pan.

In a large bowl, stir together the melted butter, milk, eggs, vanilla and 1 1/2 cups sugar substitute. Combine 3 cups of flour and baking powder; stir into the wet ingredients until just blended. Fold in the blueberries. Spread evenly in the prepared pan.

In a small bowl, stir together the brown sugar substitute, 3/4 cup of flour, and cinnamon. Stir in the softened butter with a fork until the mixture is crumbly. Sprinkle over the top of the cake.

Bake for 35 to 40 minutes in the preheated oven, until a toothpick inserted into the center of the cake comes out clean. This cake is best served warm.

Chocolate Pie

Ingredients

1/3 cup cocoa or 2 ounces unsweetened chocolate, chopped

4 teaspoons stevia (blend)

1/4 cup cornstarch

1/4 teaspoon salt

3 1/4 cups milk

1 1/2 teaspoons vanilla

1 (9 inch) baked pie shells

whipped cream

Directions

In a saucepan, mix together cocoa, stevia, cornstarch and salt. Stir milk in gradually.

Cook over medium heat, stirring constantly, until mixture boils; boil 1 minute. Remove from heat.

Blend in vanilla. Cool 10 minutes. Pour into pie shell; refrigerate.

Top with whipped cream before serving.

Chocolate Zucchini Cake

Ingredients

2 1/2 cups wheat pastry flour

1/2 cups cocoa powder

1 1/2 tsp baking powder

1 tsp baking soda

3/4 tsp salt

1 1/2 cups splenda

3 egg whites

1 whole egg

1 cup applesauce

1/3 canola oil

2 tsp. vanilla

2 cups packed grated zucchini

1 cup sugar free chocolate chips

Directions

Preheat oven to 350 prepare a 9x14 cake pan by spraying with cooking spray.

Mix top 5 ingredients together in a bowl and set aside. Mix next 7 ingredients together until well blended.

Slowly add dry ingredients to wet, while constantly mixing.

Pour into baking pan. Top with sugar free chocolate chips. Bake for 30-35 mins, or until toothpick comes out clean. Do not overbake.

Chocolate Fudge Brownies

Ingredients

2 ounces unsweetened chocolate

1 cup butter

1 **1/2** cups Splenda granular (sugar substitute)

4 large eggs

4 large egg yolks

1 tablespoon vanilla

6 tablespoons cocoa

Directions

Preheat the oven to 350 degrees.

Melt the chocolate and butter together on stovetop or in microwave. Add the Splenda, eggs, egg yolks, vanilla and cocoa, stirring until well blended.

Pour into a 9 X 13 inch pan, spray with vegetable spray and dust with cocoa.

Bake at 350F for 50 minutes.

Pumpkin Pie

Ingredients

1 (9 inch) pie shell

1 egg

6 packets granulated artificial sweetener

1 teaspoon pumpkin pie spice

1 cup pumpkin puree

1 cup evaporated milk

Directions

Preheat oven to 350 degrees F (175 degrees C).

In a medium bowl whisk together egg, sugar substitute, and pumpkin pie spice until well blended. Add pumpkin and milk to egg mixture, and stir until smooth. Pour mixture into pie shell.

Place pie on a baking sheet and bake in preheated oven for 30 minutes, or until set in center.

Coconut Cream Pie

Ingredients

1 frozen unbaked pie shell

1 (6 ounce) box sugar-free instant vanilla pudding mix

1 cup milk

1 teaspoon coconut extract

1/2 cup coconut flakes

2 (8 ounce) containers frozen whipping cream

Directions

Bake pie crust. While pie crust is baking, heat skillet and toast 1 tbsp coconut flakes until golden brown.

Mix milk, coconut extract and pudding mix together. When well blended add coconut flakes then half of whipping cream.

Once mixture is blended well pour into baked pie crust and smooth, let set for 10 minutes in refrigerator.

When ready to serve top with remaining whipping cream and toasted flakes.

Graham Cracker Chocolate Pie

Makes 2 pies

Ingredients

1 (1.4-ounce) package chocolate sugar-free, fat-free instant pudding mix

2 cups fat-free milk, divided

1 (8-ounce) container frozen reduced-calorie whipped topping, thawed

2 (6-ounce) reduced-fat graham cracker crusts

1 (1-ounce) package white chocolate sugar-free, fat-free instant pudding mix

Directions

Beat chocolate pudding mix and 1 cup milk with a mixer at medium-high speed for 3 minutes or until thickened. Gently fold in half of whipped topping.

Divide chocolate pudding mixture in half, and pour evenly into 2 graham cracker crusts.

Repeat procedure with white chocolate pudding mix, remaining 1 cup milk, and remaining half of whipped topping.

Divide mixture in half; pour over chocolate pudding mixture in both crusts. Cover and chill 3 hours or until set.

Raisin Squares

Ingredients

1 cup raisins

1/2 cup water

1/4 cup margarine

1 teaspoon cinnamon

1/2 teaspoon ground nutmeg

1 cup all-purpose flour

1 large egg, lightly beaten

3/4 cup unsweetened applesauce

Artificial sweetener, equivalent to 1 tablespoon sugar

1 teaspoon baking soda

1/4 teaspoon vanilla extract

Directions

Preheat oven to 350F.

Cook raisins, water, margarine, cinnamon and nutmeg until margarine is melted in a saucepan over medium heat for 3 minutes.

Cool, add all remaining ingredients and mix well.

Spread into an 8-inch square pan coated with nonstick cooking spray.

Bake at 350F° for 20-25 minutes or until cake appears lightly browned.

Chapter 6: Sugar Free Cookies Recipes

Peanut Butter Cookies

Ingredients

2 cups smooth natural peanut butter

2 cups Splenda

2 large eggs

Directions

Preheat oven to 350 F. Lightly grease a baking sheet.

Mix together well the peanut butter, Splenda, and eggs in a bowl. Drop mixture by spoonful balls onto the prepared baking sheet.

Bake in the preheated oven until center appears done, 8 minutes.

Oatmeal Raisin Cookies

Ingredients

1 1/2 cups rolled oats

2/3 cup butter, melted

4 egg whites

1 cup granulated artificial sweetener

1 1/2 cups all-purpose flour

1/2 teaspoon salt

2 teaspoons baking powder

1/2 cup milk

1 teaspoon vanilla extract

1/2 cup raisins

1/2 cup chopped walnuts

Directions

Preheat oven to 375 degrees F (190 degrees C). Grease cookie sheets.

Stir together the oatmeal and margarine. Blend in the egg whites and sweetener. Stir together the flour, salt and baking powder; add to the mixture alternately with the milk and vanilla; stirring between additions. Finally, stir in the raisins and walnuts.

Drop by teaspoonfuls 1 to 2 inches apart onto the prepared cookie sheets. Bake for 10 to 15 minutes in the preheated oven.

Snickerdoodles Cookies

Ingredients

1/2 cup butter

1 1/2 cup almond flour

1 cup Splenda

1 egg

1/2 tsp vanilla

1/4 tsp baking soda

1/4 tsp cream of tartar

2 tbsp splenda

1 tsp cinnamon

Directions

Mix together all top ingredients. Cover and refrigerate for 1 hour.

Mix together splenda and sugar and keep in a small dish. Roll dough into small balls and roll in splenda/cinnamon mixture.

Place on ungreased cookie sheet and cook at 350F for 12-15 minutes.

Banana Oatmeal Cookies

Ingredients

3 ripe bananas

2 cups rolled oats

1 cup dates, pitted and chopped

1/3 cup vegetable oil

1 teaspoon vanilla extract

Directions

Preheat oven to 350 degrees F (175 degrees C).

In a large bowl, mash the bananas. Stir in oats, dates, oil, and vanilla. Mix well, and allow to sit for 15 minutes. Drop by teaspoonfuls onto an ungreased cookie sheet.

Bake for 20 minutes in the preheated oven, or until lightly brown.

Chewy Pecan Cookies

Ingredients

1 1/4 cups all-purpose flour

1 teaspoon baking powder

1/4 teaspoon baking soda

1/4 teaspoon salt

1/2 cup butter or margarine

3 tablespoons brown sugar replacement

9 tablespoons Splenda

1 egg, lightly beaten

1/2 teaspoon vanilla extract

1 cup chopped pecans

Directions

Preheat the oven to 375 degrees F (190 degrees C). Sift together flour, baking powder, baking soda, and salt.

In a mixing bowl, cream together butter and sugar replacements. Beat in egg and vanilla. Mix in flour mixture. Stir in pecans. Drop by rounded teaspoon onto ungreased baking sheet.

Bake in preheated oven for about 10 minutes. Cool cookies slightly before removing from pan.

Cream Cheese Cookies

Ingredients

1 stick butter, salted (room temperature)

3 oz light cream cheese (room temperature)

1 cup flour

1 cup Splenda, granulated

Directions

Preheat oven to 350F, cover cookie sheets with parchment paper.

Cream together the butter and cream cheese in a bowl. Add flour and Splenda and mix into cream cheese mixture. Separate dough in half and make 12 small balls of dough out of each half.

Roll dough balls in the palm of your hands until smooth. flatten between palms and fingers.

Place rounds on cookie sheets and bake for 10 - 15 minutes. Cookies should be lightly brown when done.

Pumpkin Cookies

Ingredients

3/4 cup Splenda 1 teaspoon ground nutmeg

1/2 cup pumpkin puree

1 tablespoon canola oil

2 teaspoons water

2 egg whites

1 teaspoon molasses

1 tablespoon flax seeds

1 cup rolled oats

1 cup whole wheat flour

1/2 cup soy flour

1 3/4 teaspoons baking soda

1/2 teaspoon baking powder

1/2 teaspoon salt

2 teaspoons ground cinnamon

Directions

Preheat oven to 350 degrees F (175 degrees C).

In a large bowl, whisk together Splenda, oats, wheat flour, soy flour, baking soda, baking powder, salt, cinnamon, and nutmeg. Stir in pumpkin, canola oil, water, egg whites, and molasses. Stir in flax seeds, if desired. Roll into 14 large balls, and flatten on a baking sheet.

Bake for 5 minutes in preheated oven. Careful not to overbake.

Almond Cookies

Ingredients

1 stick softened butter

2 cups almond flour

1/2 cup Splenda

1 tsp vanilla extract

1 tsp almond extract

12 whole almonds

Directions

Preheat oven 300F, soften 1 stick butter add 2 cups almond flour and ½ cup Splenda to a bowl, mix well with a fork

Add vanilla and almond extract, continue to mix.

Roll into small size balls and place on lightly oiled cookie sheet. Place in oven for 5 minutes.

Remove and press down with fork in a criss cross fashion and place a whole almond in center.

Return cookies to oven for an additional 15 to 17 min remove from oven and allow to cool before transferring to a rack.

Chocolate Chip Cookies

Ingredients

1/2 cup butter, softened

3/4 cup granulated artificial sweetener

2 tablespoons water

1/2 teaspoon vanilla extract

1 egg, beaten

1 1/8 cups all-purpose flour

1/2 teaspoon baking soda

1/2 teaspoon salt

1/2 cup semisweet chocolate chips

1/2 cup chopped pecans

Directions

Preheat oven to 375 degrees F (190 degrees C).

In a medium bowl, cream together the butter and sugar substitute. Mix in water, vanilla, and egg. Sift together the flour, baking soda, and salt; stir into the creamed mixture. Mix in the chocolate chips and pecans. Drop cookies by heaping teaspoonfuls onto a cookie sheet.

Bake in the preheated oven for 10 to 12 minutes. Remove from cookie sheets to cool on wire racks.

No Bake Peanutbutter Cookies

Ingredients

1/4 cup milk

1 cup Splenda

4 tbsp butter

1 tbsp cocoa powder

1/4 cup peanut butter

1 cup oatmeal

1 tsp vanilla

Directions

Combine the first 4 ingredients in a sauce pan and bring it to a boil. Cook for 1 minute, stirring frequently, at the boil.

Remove from heat.

Add the remaining two ingredients and stir until blended.

Spoon onto wax paper and refrigerate for about 30 minutes or until firm.

Chocolate Chip Coconut Cookies

Ingredients

4 oz sugar free chocolate chips

1 oz pecans, coarsely chopped

1/4 cup unsweetened coconut, 1/2 ounce

Directions

Put the chocolate chips in a small glass bowl and microwave on MEDIUM power 1 1/2 minutes, stirring after half the time.

Stir until smooth; stir in the pecans and coconut. Drop by tablespoonfuls onto a wax paper lined baking sheet to make 12 cookies.

Chill or freeze until set. Store in the refrigerator.

Applesauce Cookies

Ingredients

1/2 cup shortening

1 egg, beaten

1/3 cup unsweetened cocoa powder

1/2 teaspoon salt

1/4 cup water

1 teaspoon baking powder

1/3 cup granulated artificial sweetener

2 cups cake flour

1/2 teaspoon ground cinnamon

1/2 teaspoon baking soda

1 cup unsweetened applesauce

Directions

Preheat oven to 375 degrees F. Grease cookie sheets.

Cream together shortening and sugar replacement. Add egg and blend well.

Sift all dry ingredients together and add alternately with applesauce and water to creamed mixture. Be sure to add flour first and last.

Drop by teaspoonfuls onto greased cookie sheets. Bake at 375F for 12-15 minutes.

Lemon Cookies

Ingredients

1/2 cup butter, softened

1/3 cup granular Splenda

1 teaspoon lemon extract

1 teaspoon vanilla

1 teaspoon lemon zest, from 1 small lemon (1 gram)

1 egg

1 cup almond flour (4 ounces)

1/3 cup vanilla whey protein powder

1 teaspoon baking powder

Directions

Put everything in a medium bowl and beat with an electric mixer until creamy. This will only take about a minute.

Using a 2 teaspoon cookie scoop, scoop 24 balls of the dough onto a silicone or parchment-lined baking sheet. Place them 6 balls across and 4 balls down on the sheet.

Cover the dough balls with a sheet of wax paper. Very gently press them down with the bottom of a glass or small bowl to about 1/4-inch thick.

Carefully remove the wax paper and bake them at 350º about 8-12 minutes or until golden brown. Cool on a wire rack.

Walnut Raisin Cookies

Ingredients

1 1/2 cups raisins

1/2 cup peeled, cored and chopped apple

1 cup water

1/2 cup butter

1 cup all-purpose flour

1 teaspoon baking soda

1 teaspoon vanilla extract

1 cup quick cooking oats

2 eggs, beaten

3/4 cup chopped walnuts

Directions

In a medium saucepan, combine the raisins, apples and water. Bring to a boil and cook for 3 minutes. Remove from heat and stir in the butter. Set aside to cool.

In a medium bowl, stir together the flour and baking soda. Stir in the vanilla, eggs and the apple mixture until well blended. Fold in the oats and nuts. Cover dough and chill 8 hours or overnight.

Preheat oven to 350F. Grease cookie sheets. Drop by rounded spoonfuls onto the prepared cookie sheet.

Bake for 8 to 10 minutes in the preheated oven. Allow cookies to cool on baking sheet for 5 minutes before removing to a wire rack to cool completely.

Conclusion

Thank you again for downloading this book!

I hope this book was able to help you to discover tasty and simple no sugar recipe ideas that you can enjoy any day of the week. Saying **goodbye to sugar** is not as hard to do as you may have imagined in the beginning. Not only have you made a lifestyle choice that will lead to you feeling better all the way around, but it will be easy to stick to now that you know how good food can taste minus the sweet.

Keep in mind that almost every food that you choose to eat has some naturally occurring sugars in them. Your body requires that it gets a certain amount to balance out all of the rest of the **nutrients**, fats, and other various things it absorbs on a daily basis.

If you yourself really craving that sweet taste of coffee, tea, or even your morning oatmeal, there are several natural sweeteners for you to choose from. I think that the best one is **liquid stevia**, all the sweet with none of the sugar. It is available at any grocery store and you will find that a little goes a long way.

Good luck on your journey down the sugar free path!

Thank you and good luck!

Part 2

Introduction

We all crave dessert – sweet, gooey, crispy, chocolaty – it's all good. Dessert may not be the healthiest part of your meal, but it sure makes the rest worthwhile. This Desserts – With Sugar and Sugar-Free Cookbook has the best of both worlds. It has yummy sugar-free desserts and desserts that use sugar. The nice thing is that you can experiment with both.

For people with diabetes or who are pre-diabetic, not eating sugar is written in stone. Your health is your main concern. But with the recipes in this Desserts – With Sugar and Sugar-Free Cookbook, you'll have plenty of delicious options. We use sugar substitutes such as Stevia and Splenda for great results. The whole family will love them, and you'll be lucky to get a small piece! Be careful using honey as a substitute. It may be nice and sweet, but it will affect your sugar level. Use raw honey instead. Some of the great recipes in this book have a bit of liqueur added for added lusciousness. Liqueur has sugar in it, so simply omit it when preparing the dessert.

If you are eating less sugar in order to lose weight, this book is for you. So many delicious recipes. You can indulge in some sugar, or you can use sugar substitutes for the same recipes for a healthier version. You can also lower the sugar content of any recipe by going half and half – half sugar and half substitute. The end result will always be delicious, sweet desserts. Be sure to use the recipes in the Dessert – With Sugar and Sugar-Free Cookbook when baking for a weight-conscious or diabetic friend. They will be so happy with your efforts.

Desserts With Sugar

Melt-In-Your-Mouth Brownies

Sweet gooey brownies are welcome any time. They always hit the spot when you crave something sweet.

Cooking Time: **30 minutes**

Servings: 6

Ingredients:

- 2 cups sugar
- 3 beaten eggs
- 2 tsp. vanilla
- ½ cup unsweetened cocoa powder
- 1 cup white flour
- Dash of salt

- ½ cup chopped walnuts
- **½ cup semi-sweet chocolate chips.**

Directions:

1. Preheat the oven to 350 degrees.

2. Lightly grease a 9 x 13 baking pan.

3. Melt the butter in the microwave or in a pan on top of the stove.

4. Remove the pan from the heat and whisk in the remaining ingredients, but don't over-stir.

5. Spoon the batter into the baking pan.

6. Bake for 30 minutes.

White Cake

Sometimes, you just want something simple and sweet. This cake is easy to prepare and is just right, with a hint of lemon.

Cooking Time:**45 minutes**

Servings: **6**

Ingredients:

- 2 eggs
- 1 ¾ cups cake flour
- 1 ¾ tsp. baking powder
- 2 tsp. vanilla extract
- ¾ cup milk
- Dash of salt
- ½ tsp. lemon extract
- **1 tsp. lemon zest**

Directions:

1. Preheat your oven to 350 degrees.

2. Lightly grease a 9x11 baking pan

3. Whisk together the sugar and butter. Add the eggs and whisk after each addition.

4. Add the vanilla, lemon extract and lemon zest.

5. In another bowl, combine the flour and baking powder

6. Add the flour to the butter mixture and stir well.

7. Slowly add the milk and keep stirring.

8. Transfer the batter to the baking pan.

9. Bake for 35-40 minutes.

Italian Cream Cake

This is a wonderful special-occasion cake. Creamy, gooey and irresistible. We're using coconut oil instead of butter because it's much healthier.

Cooking Time: **30 minutes**

Servings: **8**

Ingredients:

- 1 cup coconut oil
- 2 cups of white sugar
- 5 egg yolks – 5 egg whites
- 2 cups baking flour
- 1 tsp. of baking soda
- 1 cup buttermilk
- 1 tsp. almond extract
- 1 cup coconut flakes
- **1 cup chopped pecans**

     Icing Ingredients:
- ½ cup raspberry preserves
- 8 oz. cream cheese

- 1 tsp. vanilla extract
- 2 cups butter
- **4 cups confectioners' sugar**

Directions

1. Preheat the oven to 350 degrees.

2. Line 3 8-inch baking pans with parchment paper.

3. Grind the pecans and coconut flakes in a grinder. Set aside.

4. Whip the egg whites until they are stiff

5. In another bowl, whisk the coconut oil and sugar and they are creamy.

6. Add the egg yolks one at a time.

7. Combine the flour and baking soda.

8. Alternate adding the flour and buttermilk to the creamy mixture. Keep whisking and stirring.

9. Add the almond extract and ground pecans and coconut flakes and combine well.

10. Gently fold the stiff egg whites into the batter.

11. Transfer the batter to the prepared baking pans.

12. Bake for 30 minutes. Use a toothpick to check for doneness. Let cool.

13. For the frosting, beat the ingredients, except the raspberry preserves, with a hand mixer until creamy.

14. Lay the 3 cake layers on the counter.

15. Smear each layer with some raspberry preserve.

16. Stack the layers on top of each other and frost the top and sides.

17. If desired, you can sprinkle the top with more ground pecans.

Chocolate Eclair Cake

This is a non-bake dessert that so smooth and creamy. The rum sure adds a kick, but you can substitute another cup of milk, instead (But why?).

Cooking Time: **0**

Servings: **8**

Ingredients:
- 3 packages of graham crackers.
- 1 package vanilla pudding mix.
- 1 package cheesecake pudding mix
- 2 cups milk
- 1 cup coconut rum
- 1 cup whipped topping.
- ½ cup cocoa
- 1 cup sugar

- 1 tsp. vanilla extract
- 1 cup butter
- **¼ cup condensed milk**

Directions:

1. Place half the graham crackers on the bottom of a 9x13 dish.

2. Combine the milk, coconut rum and pudding mixes and stir in the whipped topping.

3. Spread half the mixture over the graham crackers.

4. Add the remaining crackers and top with the remaining filling.

5. Add the cocoa, sugar, vanilla, butter and milk to a sauce pan and stir until smooth.

6. Drizzle the sauce over the cake.

7. Refrigerate for at least 3 hours, preferably overnight.

Flourless Chocolate Cake

Flourless cakes are rich beyond words. We're using coffee and raspberry liqueur for a heavenly taste. Start with a small slice and work your way up.

Cooking Time: **45 minutes**

Servings: **8**

Ingredients:

- ½ cup freshly brewed strong coffee
- Dash of salt
- ¾ cup white sugar
- 1 tbsp. raspberry liqueur
- 1 cup chopped bittersweet chocolate
- 1 cup butter
- **6 eggs**

Directions

1. Preheat the oven to 300 degrees.

2. Lightly grease a 10-inch baking pan.

3. Add the coffee, salt and sugar to a small pan and heat until the sugar is dissolved. Set aside.

4. Using a bowl and melt the chocolate in the microwave.

5. Remove the melted chocolate from the microwave and add the butter 1 piece at a time.

6. Use a hand mixer to whip the chocolate and butter creamy.

7. Add the eggs and continue whipping after each addition.

8. Slowly, pour the coffee and liqueur into the mixture and combine.

9. Add the batter to the cake pan.

10. Bake the cake for 45 minutes.

Crème Brulee

This French favorite is absolutely decadent. We've actually upped the decadence by adding a bit of orange liqueur. Warning: if you serve this to guests, they will keep coming back! Freeze the egg whites for another time.

Cooking Time: **40 minutes**

Servings: **6**

Ingredients:
- 6 egg yolks
- 4 tbsp. sugar
- 1 scrapped vanilla bean
- 3 cups heavy cream

- 1 tsp. orange liqueur
- **3 tbsp. brown sugar**

Directions:

1. Preheat the oven to 300 degrees.

2. Vigorously whisk the yolks, sugar, and vanilla bean scrapings with a hand mixer.

3. Add the heavy cream to a pan and bring just to the boiling point.

4. Stir 2 tbsp. of the yolk/sugar mix into the hot cream.

5. Stir the remaining yolk/sugar mix and orange liqueur into the cream.

6. Transfer the mixture to 6 ramekins.

7. Place the ramekins on a baking sheet and place in the oven.

8. Add enough hot water to the baking sheet to halfway come up the sides of the ramekins.

9. Bake for 30 minutes.

10. Remove the baking sheet from the oven and let the crème brulee cool.

11. When ready to serve, sprinkle the top of the ramekins with the brown sugar and carefully use a small blowtorch to melt the sugar.

Chocolate Mousse

Mousse has a lighter texture than pudding. This is mousse is simply fantastic, especially since we're using Amaretto.

Cooking Time: **2 minutes**

Serving: 4

Ingredients:

- 1 cup chopped semisweet chocolate
- ¼ cup Amaretto
- 3 tbsp. salt-free butter
- 3 egg yolks
- 3 tbsp. sugar
- 1 1/3 cup whipped heavy cream
- **1 tsp. vanilla extract**

Directions:

1. Combine the chocolate, Amaretto and butter in a bowl.

2. Microwave the mixture until the chocolate melts and you have a creamy mix. Let cool.

3. Whisk the egg yolks and sugar with 4 tbsp. of water and pour into a small pan.

4. Cook on the lowest possible heat for 2 minutes to reach 160 degrees. Use a candy thermometer, if possible. It's critical that the yolks don't "scramble."

5. Remove the pan from the stove and stir in the chocolate mixture.

6. Place the pan on a platter of ice for 10 minutes.

7. Combine the whipped cream and vanilla and fold into the mousse.

8. Transfer the moose into 4 separate dishes and refrigerate overnight.

Madeleines

Madeleines are a delicious cookie-cake. They are perfect for when you don't want something overly sweet. And you really want to enjoy them with a nice cup of coffee. Baking madeleines requires a madeleine pan. If you don't have one, you can use a cake pan and create a cake with the same flavor and texture.

Cooking Time: **10 minutes**

Servings: **12**

Ingredients:

- 2 eggs
- ½ cup sugar
- 6 tbsp. unsalted butter
- 1 cup flour
- 1 tsp. baking powder
- 3 tbsp. orange zest
- **½ tbsp. vanilla extract**

Directions:

1. Whip the eggs and sugar in a bowl with a hand mixer.

2. Slowly add the flour, baking powder, orange zest and vanilla.

3. Melt the butter in a pan and stir into the mixture.

4. Place a towel on top of the bowl and let rest for 1 hour.

5. Preheat the oven to 375 degrees.

6. Lightly grease a madeleine pan.

7. Spoon the batter into the madeleine molds

8. Bake for 10 minutes.

Note: Some cooks like to dust the madeleines with confectioner's sugar after baking. That's your choice.

Fruit Clafouti

Clafouti is somewhere between a pie and a custard. Plums are a bit tangy, so this dish screams for a whipped topping or ice cream.

Cooking Time: **1 hour**

Servings: **6**

Ingredients:

- 6 tbsp. sugar
- 1 lb. plums
- 2 peaches
- 3 eggs
- 1 cup milk
- ¼ cup heavy cream
- 2/3 cup white flour
- 2 tsp. vanilla
- 1 tbsp. brandy
- Dash of salt
- ½ tsp. cinnamon

- **2 tbsp. confectioners' sugar**

Directions:

1. Preheat the oven to 375 degrees.

2. Lightly grease a 10-inch pie pan.

3. Thinly slice both the plums and peaches and place inside the pie pan with the cut side facing down.

4. Drizzle with 2 tbsp. sugar.

5. Combine the remaining ingredients in a blender to a smooth consistency.

6. Pour the custard over the fruit.

7. Bake the caflouti for 1 hour.

8. Sprinkle with the confectioner's sugar and serve with whipped topping or ice cream.

Tiramisu

This is serious tiramisu. The Kahlua-infused brushed ladyfingers are so good.

Cooking Time: **15 minutes**

Servings: **8**

Ingredients:

- 6 egg yolks
- 1 cup sugar
- 1 cup cream cheese
- 2¼ cup heavy whipping cream
- 4 tbsp. sour cream
- 1 package ladyfingers
- **¼ cup coffee and Kahlua or rum mixture**

Directions:

1. Using a double boiler, whisk the egg yolks and sugar for 10 minutes, until smooth.

2. Remove from the double boiler and keep stirring for 5 more minutes.

3. In a bowl, combine the cream cheese, ¼ cup heavy cream, and the sour cream until smooth.

4. Add the mixture to the egg yolks and beat well.

5. In another bowl, whip up the remaining heavy cream and gently stir into the egg yolk mixture.

6. Brush the ladyfingers with the coffee/Kahlua mixture.

7. Cut the ladyfingers in half.

8. Cover the bottom of a bowl with lady fingers and drizzle with more of the coffee/Kahlua mixture and top with half the filling.

9. Add another layer of ladyfingers and a layer of filling.

10. If desired, garnish with a few chocolate curls.

Italian Cheese Cake:

This cheesecake uses ricotta cheese instead of all cream cheese. It's lightly and a heavenly treat.

Cooking Time: 1 hour 10 minutes

Servings: **8**

Ingredients:

- 1 lb. quality ricotta cheese
- 1 cup cream cheese
- 2 tbsp. ground hazelnuts
- 1 cup sugar
- ½ cup white flour
- 6 eggs
- ¼ cup Amaretto
- 2 tsp. almond extract
- Dash of salt
- **1 cup sour cream**

Directions

1. Preheat the oven to 475 degrees.

2. Grease a springform pan.

3. Drain the ricotta cheese of liquid by wrapping it in cheese cloth and placing it in a colander. Wring out all excess liquid.

4. Combine the ricotta and cream cheese and blend well.

5. Add the eggs one at a time and combine well.

6. Stir in the remaining ingredients, the sour cream last.

7. Transfer the batter to the springform pan.

8. Bake for 10 minutes

9. Reduce the temperature to 200 degrees and bake for another 1 hour.

10. Turn off oven and let sit for 2 hours.

11. Allow to chill before slicing.

German Apple Strudel

Wonderful strudel. Your guests will be so impressed. Serve with a good cup of coffee.

Cooking Time: **40 minutes**

Servings: **6**

Ingredients:

- 3 thinly sliced apples
- 3 tbsp. honey
- 1 tsp. cinnamon
- ½ tsp. allspice
- 1 tbsp flour
- ¼ cup chopped walnuts
- ½ lb. package of thawed frozen phyllo dough
- **1 egg white**

Directions:

1. Preheat the oven to 375 degrees.

2. Grease a baking sheet and dust with flour.

3. Combine the sliced apples, honey, cinnamon, allspice, flour and chopped nuts in a bowl.

4. Spread the frozen dough on a flat surface.

5. Spoon the filling onto the dough, leaving a generous border.

6. Roll up the dough and secure the ends.

7. Place the strudel on the baking sheet.

8. Mix the egg white and 4 tbsp. of water and brush over the entire strudel.

9. Bake for 40 minutes.

10. Let cool before slicing

Baklava

The great thing about baklava (besides the wonderful sweet taste) is that it looks complicated, and people think you're Martha Steward reincarnate when you serve it. It's so impressive. It is a bit time-consuming, but it's fairly easy to prepare. And definitely worth the effort.

Cooking Time: **50 minutes**

Servings: **12**

Ingredients:
- 1 package phyllo dough
- 1 lb. chopped walnuts and pistachios
- ¼ cup sugar
- 1 ½ tsp. cinnamon
- 1 cup melted butter
- 1 cup sugar
- ¾ cup honey
- **1 tbsp. lemon zest**

Directions:

1. Preheat the oven to 350 degrees.
2. Lightly grease a 9 x13 baking dish.
3. Make sure the nuts are finely chopped, then toss with cinnamon and ¼ cup sugar.
4. Place the phyllo dough on a flat surface and cut in half.
5. Place a damp towel over the phyllo as your work with it.
6. Lay 2 phyllo sheets in the baking dish and brush with the melted butter.
7. Spoon some nut filling onto each layer.
8. Repeat the layering to create 8 layers.
9. Cut the baklava into diamond shapes.
10. Bake for 50 minutes.
11. While the baklava bakes, combine the sugar, honey, lemon zest and 1 cup of water in a pan.
12. Simmer the sauce for 15 minutes.
13. Pour the sauce over the baklava when it is done and allow to cool.

Almond Cookies

You love those almond cookies in Chinese bakeries. Now, you can bake them yourself.

Cooking Time: **10 cookies**

Servings: 12 minutes

Ingredients:

- 1 ¾ cup flour
- 1 cup sugar
- ½ tsp. baking soda
- Dash of salt
- 1 cup butter (or half butter, half Crisco)
- ¾ cup ground almonds or walnuts
- 1 tbsp. Frangelico liqueur
- 1 beaten egg
- **1 tsp. almond extract**

Directions:

1. Preheat the oven to 325 degrees.

2. Combine the flour, sugar, baking soda and salt in a bowl.

3. Cut the butter into the mixture to get a grainy texture.

4. Stir in the ground nuts, liqueur, egg and almond extract and combine well.

5. Create 1-inch balls and place them on a cookie sheet.

6. Flatten the balls with a fork.

7. If desired, top each cookie with a slivered almond.

8. Bake for 12 minutes.

Peach Cobbler

So easy to prepare and so good. To make this dish sugar-free, just substitute the sugar with Truvia brown sugar replacement. Use fresh peaches, if possible. If they're not available, used canned peaches and adjust the sugar.

Cooking Time: **55 minutes**

Servings: **6**

Ingredients:

- 8 peeled and sliced peaches
- 2 cups white sugar (if using canned peaches, reduce to 1 cup sugar
- ½ tsp. cinnamon
- ¼ tsp. nutmeg
- ½ tsp. lemon juice
- 1 cup flour
- ¼ tsp. baking soda
- ½ cup milk
- **½ cup melted butter**

Directions:

1. If using fresh peaches, combine with 1 cup of sugar and 1 cup of water in a pan.

2. Bring the water to a boil, then simmer for 10 minutes.

3. If using canned peaches, retain the syrup and simmer for 10 minutes.

4. Combine the sugar, cinnamon, nutmeg, lemon juice, baking powder and flour.

5. Stir in the milk until you have a batter.

6. Pour the melted butter in a baking dish.

7. Top evenly with the batter.

8. Spoon the cooked peaches over the batter.

9. Don't stir anything while you are assembling the cobbler.

10. Bake for 45 minutes.

Strawberry Shortcake

It's Spring, and the strawberries are ripe and lush. It's time for strawberry shortcake! This shortcake has a biscuit-type base. You can prepare a whole cake or make individual shortcakes by creating biscuit-sized pieces.

Cooking Time: **20 minutes**

Servings: **8**

Ingredients:

- 6 cups washed and sliced strawberries
- 1/3 cup sugar
- 2 ¼ cups white flour
- 2 tsp. baking powder
- 3 tbsp. sugar
- Dash of salt
- ½ cup butter
- 1 beaten egg
- ¾ cups milk
- **1 ½ cup whipped cream (for a real treat, whip up some real heavy cream with a tbsp. of sugar)**

Directions:

1. Toss the strawberries with the 1/3 cup sugar and let site for at least an hour.

2. Preheat the oven to 425 degrees.

3. Lightly great an 8-inch cake pan and drizzle with flour.

4. Combine 2 ¼ cup flour, baking powder, 3 tbsp. sugar and salt in a bowl.

5. Use a pastry blender to cut in the butter until the mixture is quite coarse.

6. Add the egg and milk and stir to combine. Don't over-stir.

7. Pour the batter into the cake pan.

8. Bake for 20 minutes. (If baking biscuits, bake for 13-14 minutes)

9. When the cake is cool enough to cut, slice it in half.

10. Cover one half with the strawberries, top with second half, and cover with remaining strawberries.

11. Top the strawberry shortcake with whipped cream.

Chocolate Soufflé

A soufflé impresses everyone. This one is easy to prepare and slightly decadent with the addition of the coffee liqueur.

Cooking Time 25 **minutes:**

Servings: **4**

Ingredients:
- 3 tbsp. butter
- 1 tbsp. unsweetened cocoa powder
- 4 tbsp. sugar
- 2 tbsp. flour
- ¾ cup milk
- 4 eggs, separated into yolks and whites
- ½ tsp. scrapped vanilla bean
- 2 tbsp. coffee liqueur
- 2 tbsp. expresso coffee
- 2 tbsp. semi-bitter chocolate chips.
- ½ cup raspberries
- **2 tbsp. melted semisweet chocolate chips**

Directions

1. Preheat the oven to 400 degrees.
2. Grease the bottom of 4 ramekins with 1 tbsp. butter.
3. Combine the cocoa powder and 2 tbsp. of sugar.
4. In another bowl, stir the butter into the flour.
5. Beat 1 egg yolk in a third bowl
6. Bring the milk just to boiling in a pan and briskly stir in the butter/flour paste until the butter is totally melted.
7. Whip the milk mixture into the yolk.
8. Return the milk/egg yolk to the pan and simmer for 2 minutes while stirring.
9. Remove the custard from the stove.

10. In a separate bowl, whisk 3 egg yolks, vanilla bean, coffee liqueur, expresso together.

11. Stir the mixture into the cocoa powder mixture.

12. Whisk the cocoa powder mixture in the custard and set aside.

13. Whisk the egg white until they peak.

14. Add 3 tbsp. of sugar and keep whipping.

15. Gently fold the egg whites into the custard.

16. Fill the ramekins with the custard.

17. Bake for 20 minutes.

18. While the soufflés are baking, mash the raspberries using a hand mixer and stir in the melted chocolate chips.

19. Drizzle the raspberry sauce over the soufflé.

Pecan Pie

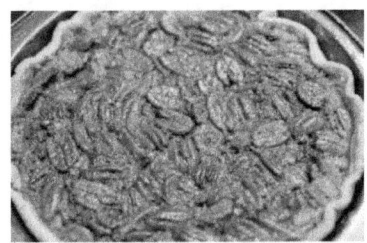

A pecan pie with attitude. You don't have to add the bourbon, but why not? It gives the pie something special. And, it's so important to toast the pecans to bring out all their flavor. This will be a holiday must-have at your table.

Cooking Time: 1 hour 15 minutes

Servings: **8**

Ingredients:

- ½ cup Karo light corn syrup
- ½ cup of Karo dark corn syrup
- 1 cup sugar
- 3 eggs
- 2 tbsp. melted butter
- ¼ cup bourbon
- 1 1/2 cups pecans
- **1 unbaked pie crust**

Directions:

1. Place the pecans in a skillet and toast for 5-6 minutes. Shake the skillet occasionally to keep the nuts from sticking. Set aside.

2. Combine the remaining ingredients in a bowl.

3. Add the toasted pecans.

4. Transfer the filling to the unbaked pie crust.

5. Bake at 350 degrees for 1 hour 10 minutes.

6. Let cool before servings.

Coconut Cream Pie

This pie is rich – we're talking little Greek who owns his own island-type rich. The coconut cream does have fat and sugar, but it adds a lot of immune system and anti-aging benefits. For less calories (and less richness) use coconut milk.

Cooking Time: **2 minutes**

Servings: **8**

Ingredients:

- 1 cup sweetened flaked coconut

- 1 15-oz. can coconut cream
- 1 cup half and half
- 3 egg yolks
- 1 cup white sugar
- ½ cup cornstarch
- Dash of salt
- 1 tsp. coconut extract
- 1 thawed frozen pie shell
- **Whipped cream for topping**

Directions:

1. Preheat your oven to 350 degrees.

2. Place the coconut flakes on a baking sheet and then toast them in the oven for 5 minutes. Set aside.

3. Combine the coconut milk, half and half, egg yolks, sugar, cornstarch and salt in a small pan and stir.

4. Bring the liquid to a boil, then reduce the heat to low while stirring for 2 minutes.

5. Remove the pan from the stove and add ¾ cup toasted coconut flakes and coconut extract.

6. Pour the filling into the pie sheet and refrigerate for 6 hours.

7. Top with whipped cream and remaining coconuts.

Chocolate Gingerbread Cookies

The classic gingerbread cookie is kicked up a notch with some chocolate. Who could resist?

Cooking Time: **8 minutes**

Servings: 20 cookies

Ingredients:

- 1 ½ white flour
- 1 tbsp. Dutch cocoa
- 1 tsp. baking powder
- 2 tsps. ground ginger
- ½ tsp. nutmeg
- ¼ tsp. salt
- ½ cup brown sugar
- 1 cup butter
- 2 tbsp. molasses
- 1 cup chopped dark chocolate
- 1/3 cup chopped crystallized ginger
- **¼ cup light brown sugar**

Directions:

1. Preheat the oven to 325 degrees.

2. Line 2 baking sheets with a parchment paper.

3. Combine the flour, baking powder, ginger, nutmeg, cocoa powder and salt in a bowl.

4. In a separate bowl, whip the brown sugar and butter with a hand mixer until it is creamy. Add the molasses and whip until combined.

5. Add the flour and stir thoroughly.

6. Stir in the chopped chocolate and crystalized ginger and gently mix just to combine. Don't overmix.

7. Use a tablespoon to scoop out a ball of dough.

8. Place the balls on the baking sheets.

9. Flatten the cookies with a spatula.

10. Dust with the light brown sugar.

11. Bake for 8 minutes and check for doneness.

Sugar-Free Desserts

Sugar Free Strawberry Cheesecake

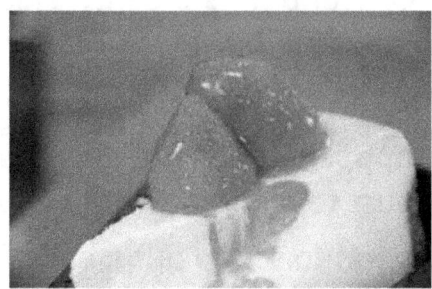

No baking and no sugar. Just a delicious cheesecake.

Cooking Time: **0**

Servings: **6**

Ingredients:

- 1 sugar-free graham cracker crust
- 1 package cream cheese
- 4 tbsp. sour cream
- 1 ¼ cups evaporated milk
- 1 tsp. vanilla extract
- 1 package sugar-free vanilla pudding
- **2 cups washed and sliced strawberries**

Direction:

1. Whip the cream cheese with a hand mixer until smooth.

2. Add the milk and sour cream and continue mixing on low.

3. Stir in the vanilla extract and vanilla pudding and combine.

4. Transfer the filling to the graham cracker crust.

5. Arrange the strawberry slices on top.

6. Refrigerate the cheesecake for 2 or more hours.

Cinnamon Coffee Cake

There's nothing like a good coffee cake, either for dessert or anytime with a good cup of coffee. Why not make it even better by omitting the sugar?

Cooking Time: **40 minutes**

Servings: **6**

Ingredients:
- 1 cup melted butter
- 1 cup milk

- 4 eggs
- 1 tsp. of vanilla extract
- 1 ¼ cups Stevia or Splenda sweetener
- 3 cups white flour
- 2 tsp. of baking powder
- **½ tsp. baking soda**
- 1 cup chopped walnuts
- 1 ½ cups Truvia brown sugar substitute
- ¾ cup flour
- 2 tsp. cinnamon
- **1/3 cup butter**

Directions:

1. Preheat the oven to 350 degrees.

2. Coat a 9x13 baking dish with non-stick spray.

3. Whisk together the butter, milk, eggs, vanilla and sweetener.

4. Combine the flour, baking powder and baking soda and add the flour to the milk mixture.

5. Evenly distribute the batter in the baking dish.

6. In a bowl, combine the chopped nuts, Truvia, flour and cinnamon. Add the butter until you have a crumbly texture.

7. Add the topping to the batter.

8. Bake for 40 minutes.

Pumpkin Pie

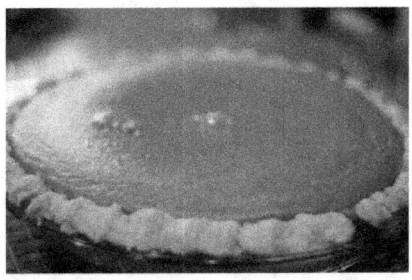

Pumpkin pie is a holiday tradition, and this is the perfect pie for anyone avoiding sugar.

Cooking Time: **55 minutes**

Servings: **8**

Ingredients:

- 2 cups pumpkin pie filling
- 2 eggs
- 1/3 cup Splenda or Stevia sweetener
- Dash of salt
- 1 tsp. pumpkin pie spice
- 1 cup condensed milk
- ¼ tsp. nutmeg
- **1 frozen pastry shell**

Directions:

1. Stir together the pumpkin pie filling, eggs, sweetener, salt, pumpkin spice and condensed milk until creamy and smooth.

2. Fill the pie shell with the filling.

3. Bake for 15 minutes at 425 degrees.

4. Lower the temperature to 350 degrees and bake for 40 minutes.

Honey Cake

A moist honey cake really hits the spot.

Cooking Time: **45 minutes**

Servings: **8**

Ingredients:
- 1 cup Stevia and Splenda sweetener
- 1 cup raw honey or agave nectar
- ½ cup coconut oil
- 4 eggs
- 1 tbsp. lemon zest
- 1 cup coffee
- 2 ½ cup flour
- 3 tsp. baking powder
- ½ tsp. baking soda

- Dash of salt
- **1 tsp. cinnamon**

Directions:

1. Preheat the oven to 350 degrees.

2. Lightly butter a 9x13 inch cake pan.

3. Combine flour, baking powder, baking soda, salt and cinnamon in a bowl.

4. Use a second bowl and add the sweetener, honey or agave nectar, coconut oil, eggs and lemon zest.

5. Add the flour mixture to the honey mixture while adding the coffee a bit at a time.

6. Spread the batter even into the cake pan.

7. Bake for 45 minutes and let cool.

Chocolate Pie

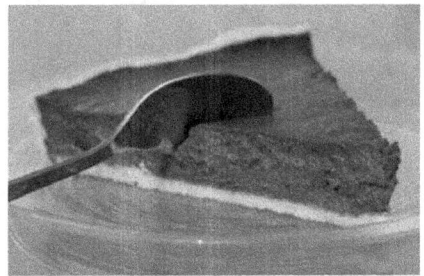

This sugar-free chocolate pie is so much better than the usual, as we've tweaked the filling for more flavor.

Cooking Time: **5 minutes**

Servings: **8**

Ingredients:

- 2 package instant sugar-free pudding mix
- 3 ¼ cup milk
- ½ cup evaporated milk
- 1 tbsp. unsweetened cocoa powder
- 1 tbsp. Splenda sweetener
- Dash of vanilla extract
- 1 tsp. butter
- **¼ cup sugar-free whipped cream**

Directions:

1. Add the pudding mix, milk, evaporated milk, cocoa powder, sweetener to a pan and bring to a boil while continuously stirring.

2. Remove from stove when the mixture has thickened – 1 or 2 minutes.

3. Stir in the vanilla and butter and pour the filling into the pie crust.

4. Refrigerate for 2 hours.

5. If desired, top with whipped cream.

Raspberry Custard

A creamy custard with no sugar for the whole family.

Cooking Time: **45 minutes**

Servings 6:

Ingredients:

- 3 eggs
- 2 cups washed raspberries
- ½ tsp. cinnamon
- ½ tsp. baking powder
- ½ tsp. coconut extract
- ½ cup slivered almonds
- **1/3 cup flour**

Directions:

1. Whip the eggs and raspberries in a blender until smooth

2. Add the remaining ingredients and process.

3. Fill 6 ramekins with the custard ingredients and place on a baking sheet.

4. Place the baking sheet in the oven and pour an inch of hot water onto the baking sheet.

5. Bake for 45 minutes.

6. Let the custard cool before serving.

Funnel Cake

Frankly, we're hoping for a bit of applause for this one. Funnel cake with no sugar AND fried in heart-healthy coconut oil? Yes! If you don't have a kitchen funnel, just use a clean squeeze bottle or zip-lock bag.

Cooking Time: 3 minutes each

Servings: **6**

Ingredients:
- 2 cups white flour
- 1 tsp. baking powder
- ¾ tsp. salt
- 1 cup Stevia or Splenda – divided

- 2 eggs
- 1 ½ cups milk
- ½ tsp. vanilla extract
- 2 cups coconut oil
- **¾ tsp. cornstarch**

Directions:

1. Combine the flour, baking powder, salt and ¼ cup Splenda in a blender and process.

2. Whisk the eggs, milk and vanilla in a bowl.

3. Stir the flour mixture into the egg mixture.

4. Sift together the flour, baking powder, and salt.

5. Heat the coconut oil in a skillet until it is very hot.

6. Fill whatever type funnel you are using with ½ cup batter.

7. Squeeze the batter into the hot oil.

8. Drain the funnel cake on a paper towel.

9. Repeat with the remaining batter.

10. Place ¾ cup Stevia and the cornstarch in a blender and process to create confectioner's sugar.

11. Dust the funnel cakes with the confectioner's sugar.

Banana Cake With Frosting

Cake with frosting! How great is that? No sugar anywhere, and this banana cake is beyond delicious. If you want a plainer frosting, you can omit the cocoa powder.

Cooking Time: **30 minutes**

Servings: **8**

Ingredients:

- 2 cups cake flour
- 1 tsp. cinnamon
- 1 tsp. baking powder
- ½ tsp. baking soda
- 2 ripe bananas
- ½ cup sour cream
- ⅓ cup agave nectar
- ½ tsp. salt
- 1 tsp. vanilla extract
- 2 tbsp. melted butter
- 1 egg
- **1 cup chopped walnuts**

Frosting Ingredients:

- ¾ cup unsweetened cocoa powder

- ½ cup coconut oil
- ½ cup agave nectar
- **1 tsp. vanilla extract**

Directions:

1. Preheat the oven to 350 degrees.

2. Lightly grease an 8-inch cake pan.

3. Combine the flour, baking powder, baking soda, salt and cinnamon in a bowl.

4. Use a hand mixer or blender to whip the bananas, sour cream, vanilla, butter and egg creamy.

5. Add the banana mixture to the flour and combine well.

6. Fold in the chopped walnuts

7. Transfer the batter to the cake pan and bake for 30 minutes.

8. To prepare the frosting, place the frosting ingredients in a blender and whip to creamy smoothness.

9. When cake has cooled, spread the frosting on the sides and top.

Peanut Butter Cookies

These cookies are great anytime, and no one has to know they don't contain sugar.

Cooking Time: **9-10 minutes**

Servings: **20**

Ingredients:

- 2 cups organic peanut butter – either smooth or crunchy or a mix thereof.
- 1/3 cup rolled oats
- 1 ½ cup Splenda or Stevia
- 1/3 cup agave nectar
- ¼ cup unsweetened cocoa powder
- 1 tsp. vanilla extract
- **2 eggs**

Directions:

1. Preheat the oven to 350 degrees.
2. Coat a baking sheet with non-stick spray.

3. Combine all ingredients in a bowl and incorporate well.

4. Use a tablespoon to drop the dough onto the baking sheet.

5. Bake for 9-10 minutes.

6. Cookies will be crumbly after baking, so let sit for 1 hour.

Fruit Mousse

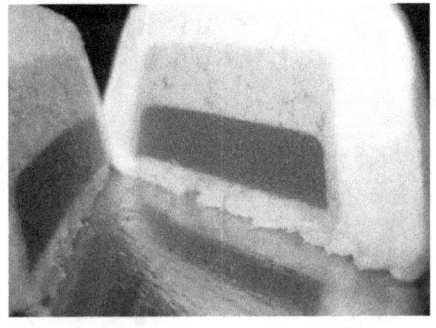

The sweetness comes from the fruits, so enjoy as much as you want.

Cooking Time: **0**

Servings: **2**

Ingredients:
- 1 mango
- 1 cup frozen raspberries
- 1 cup pineapple bits

- 1 cup sugar-free whipped topping
- **1/3 cup condensed milk**

Directions:

1. Whip the ingredients in a blender until smooth.
2. Pour the mousse into individual glasses or bowls.
3. If desired, top with fresh raspberries.

Lemon Pie

A nice, tangy pie sweetened by the whipped cream.

Cooking Time: **30 minutes**

Servings: **8**

Ingredients:

- 1 frozen pie crust
- 4 eggs

- ½ cup Stevia or Splenda sweetener
- ½ cup sour cream
- Dash of salt
- 2/3 cup lemon juice
- 1 cup sugar-free whipped cream
- **2 tbsp. lemon zest**

Directions:

1. Preheat the oven to 350 degrees.

2. Combine the eggs, sweetener, sour cream and salt in a bowl.

3. Use a hand mixer to add the lemon juice.

4. Transfer the filling to the pie crust.

5. Bake for 30 minutes.

6. Whisk together the whipped topping and lemon zest and spread on top of the pie.

Ginger Cookies

Great cookies that aren't too sweet.

Cooking Time: **15 minutes**

Servings: 16 cookies

- 2 cup white flour
- 1/3 cup coconut oil
- 1 egg
- 3 tbsp. grated ginger
- 1 tsp. cinnamon
- ½ tsp. of nutmeg
- ½ tsp. cloves
- ¾ cup Stevia or Splenda sweetener
- **Dash of salt**

Directions:

1. Preheat the oven to 350 degrees.
2. Combine the ingredients in a bowl.
3. Coat a baking sheet with non-stick spray.
4. Use a tablespoon to drop dough on baking sheet.
5. Bake for 15 minutes.

Coconut Truffles

Real truffles without sugar. Just gobble them up, because someone else will.

Cooking Time: **0**

Servings: **10**

Ingredients:

- 1/2 cup coconut butter
- 4 tbsp. unsweetened cocoa powder
- 1 tbsp. sugar-free Kahlua liqueur
- 1 tbsp. coconut flakes
- 1 tsp. agave nectar
- **1 tbsp. coconut oil**

Directions:

1. Place the coconut butter in a microwave for a few seconds until it melts.

2. Combine the coconut butter with the remaining ingredients except the coconut oil.

3. Drizzle the coconut oil on the bottom of each ice cube tray cup.

4. Spoon some truffle mixture into each cup and lightly press down.

5. Place in refrigerator for 5 hours.

6. Defrost the truffles and serve.

Chocolate Lava Cake

A cake that literally bursts with sugar-free molten chocolate. So much fun, while also delicious and healthy.

Cooking Time: **15 minutes**

Servings: **6**

Directions:

- 1 cup 80 percent plus chocolate
- ¼ cup coconut oil
- 5 eggs
- 2 egg yolk
- 2 tbsp. Splenda or Stevia sweetener
- ¾ cup white flour
- **¼ cup milk**

Directions:

1. Preheat oven to 400 degrees.

2. Lightly butter 6 ramekins.

3. Place the chocolate and coconut oil in a saucepan and keep stirring until creamy and smooth. Set aside.

4. Whisk the eggs and yolks and sweetener together.

5. Stir in the flour until you have a smooth consistency.

6. Heat the milk in a second pan, but don't bring to a boil.

7. Drizzle the milk into the eggs and keep stirring vigorously.

8. Slowly at the melted chocolate.

9. Transfer the batter to the ramekins.

10. Bake for 15 minutes. Check after 10-12 minutes.

11. Serve while hot.

Banana Nut Bread

You can eat this super-moist bread anytime. If you want to, you can switch carob chips for the nuts. Or use both.

Cooking Time: **10**

Servings: **1 hour**

Ingredients:

- ⅓ cup melted coconut oil
- ½ cup raw honey
- 2 eggs
- 2 mashed bananas
- ¼ cup coconut milk
- 1 teaspoon baking soda
- 1 teaspoon vanilla extract
- ½ teaspoon salt
- **½ cup chopped walnuts**

Directions:

1. Preheat the oven to 325 degrees.

2. Spray a 9x15 loaf pan with non-stick spray.

3. Whisk the coconut oil and raw honey together.

4. Beat in the eggs, then the mashed bananas and coconut milk

5. Stir in the baking soda and salt.

6. Add the flour and nuts, but don't over-stir.

7. Transfer the batter to the loaf pan.

8. Bake for 60 minutes.

Cherry Pie

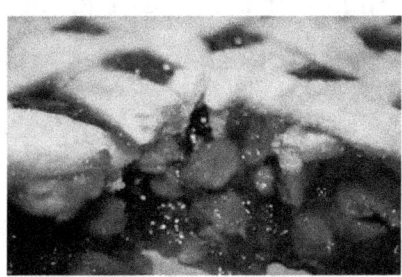

Preparing this cherry pie couldn't be easier. And the results couldn't be tastier. Top with sugar-free whipped cream.

Cooking Time: **50 minutes**

Servings: **8**

Ingredients:

- 2 frozen pie crusts
- 1 cup Stevia or Splenda sweetener
- ¼ cup cornstarch
- 4 cups pitted cherries – frozen or fresh
- ½ teaspoon vanilla extract
- **½ tsp. lemon juice**

Directions:

1. Preheat the oven to 400 degrees.

2. Combine the sweetener and cornstarch and heat in a small pan.

3. Stir in the cherries and keep stirring to thicken the filling.

4. Add the vanilla extract and lemon juice.

5. Remove the pan and allow to cool.

6. Transfer the filling into one of the pie crusts.

7. Top with the second crust; cut 4-5 slits into the top crust.

8. Bake for 50 minutes. The crust should be nice and brown.

Pineapple Upside-Down Cake

This sugar-free upside-down cake is remarkably moist with the addition of sour cream. Everyone will be in line for seconds.

Cooking Time: **35 minutes**

Servings: **8**

Ingredients:

- 2 tbsp. butter
- ½ cup Truvia brown sugar substitute
- 1 large can pineapple slices with juices
- 8 drained maraschino cherries

- 2 cups white flour
- ¾ cup Splenda or Splenda sweetener
- 1 ½ teaspoons baking powder
- ¼ tsp. of salt
- ½ cup softened butter
- 3 beaten eggs
- ¼ cup sour cream
- ¼ cup evaporated milk
- 3 tbsp. pineapple juice
- **1 teaspoon vanilla**

Directions:

1. Preheat the oven to 350 degrees.

2. Melt the butter in a span and stir in the brown sweetener and combine.

3. Add the pineapple slices and cherries and set aside.

4. In a bowl, stir together the flour, sweetener, baking powder and salt.

5. Slice in the butter with a pastry blender under the texture is crumbly.

6. In second bowl, combine the sour cream, 3 tbsp. pineapple juice, eggs and vanilla.

7. Using a hand mixer to add the sour cream mixture to the flour until creamy.

8. Transfer the pineapples and cherries to a baking pan.

9. Smooth the batter over the fruit.

10. Bake for 35 minutes.

11. Let the cake cool before inverting onto a plate.

Shortbread Cookies

Shortbread cookies are simple and utterly delightful.

Cooking Time: **25 minutes**

Serves 15

Ingredients:

- 2 cups flour
- 1/3 Stevia or Splenda sweetener
- Dash of salt
- ¾ cup butter
- **½ cup ground hazelnuts**

Directions:

1. Place all ingredients in a blender and process.

2. Roll the dough into a tube and freeze for at least an hour.

3. Remove the dough and slice into cookies.

4. Coat a baking sheet with non-stick spray and add the cookies.

5. Bake at 350 degrees for 25 minutes.